Spiritual Lessons from the Journeys of the Pilgrim

Father Raphael

Spiritual Lessons from the Journeys of the Pilgrim

Copyright©2007-2011 Father Raphael.

Published by Saint Flannan's Communion

c/o McGallen & Bolden PR Corporation.

ISBN-13: 978-0-615-45450-4

1. Bible. Interpretation, commentary. 2. Theology. 3. Prayer. 4. Orthodox Christianity. I. Phan, Seamus. II. Title.

987654321 Printed in the United States of America

With gratitude

This unworthy servant would like to thank: God, the most Holy Theotokos, the many great saints before us who inspired us with the writings, the anonymous pilgrim of "The Way of a Pilgrim", hierarchs of the Church, fellow pastoral laborers of Christ, and the families. The road is long, and sometimes rocky, but it is such a rewarding journey joyously shared by so many wonderful people. Thank you!

Table of Contents

Introduction

Dear beloved,

Welcome to this pocketbook on some humble and personal reflections on "The Way of a Pilgrim". The book touched me personally and spiritually, and I hope you can walk with us this humble pilgrimage through the Prayer of the Heart. We are very blessed and grateful to be allowed to participate in this month-long exercise, by the kind invitation of Father John Peck of the Preachers Institute (between November 15 to December 25, 2010).

About "The Way of a Pilgrim"

A 19th century Russian Orthodox pilgrim travels around Russia in search of unceasing and interior prayer, basing on insights from clergy, the Holy Bible, and the Philokalia (Greek for "love of the beautiful").

There are two books, "The Way of a Pilgrim", and "The Pilgrim Continues his Way". The pilgrim finds tremendous solace and insight into the prayer of the heart, or the Jesus Prayer.

The Philokalia in brief

The Philokalia embodies a collection of wisdom texts from contemplative, ascetic and hesychast masters from Eastern Orthodox, Oriental Orthodox and Latin traditions, ranging from 4th to 15th centuries. Saint Nikodemos of the Holy Mountain Athos and Saint Makarios of Corinth compiled the collection in the 18th century.

Some of the writers include great saints before us, including: Saint John Cassian the Roman, Saint Mark the Ascetic, Saint John of Karpathos, Saint Maximos the Confessor, Saint John of Damascus, Saint Symeon the New Theologian, Saint Gregory Palamas, etc.

There are 5 volumes in total, of which only the first 4 volumes have been translated into English. The 5th volume is only available in Greek, including writers such as Kallistos, Ignatios the Xanthopouloses, Kallistos Angelikoudis, Saint Simeon of Thessaloniki, Saint Mark the Gentle, Saint Symeon the New Theologian, Saint Gregory of Sinai, etc.

Why a study of "The Way of a Pilgrim"?

I guess it all started in 2004, when I was in the darkest of hours, with not many people to turn to. It was then, God lent His mercy by alleviating my selfish suffering, and turned me to laboring alongside some godly clergy, for humanitarian causes. Through them, I found my way back to Christ, and God called me to vocation. The book "The Way of a Pilgrim", very much resonated with me as I embraced the same journey. Though I am but a grave sinner on the beginnings of what I pray and hope to be a lifelong joyous journey, nonetheless, I sincerely hope you and I can share our journey together. Through this book, I hope you will also find the exquisite beauty of the many saints in the Philokalia, which is an illuminating book mentioned in "The Way of a Pilgrim".

Someone said, "The Way of a Pilgrim" and "The Pilgrim continues his way", are esoteric and complex. I would suggest that both books, though complex, are like onions. You peel away layer by layer, the deeper and deeper you approach them. I have approached both books simply, as the wisdom along in the outer layers of the books, are sufficient for me to find much solace and wisdom from. Sometimes, it may be tempting to dwell deep into theology, and forget that the most important theology is simple, honest prayer. Let us remember Evagrius Ponticus who said, "If you are a theologian, you will pray truly. And if you pray truly, you are a theologian."

We based our journey with the book using Olga Savin's English translation. We went through both "The Way of a Pilgrim" and "The Pilgrim Continues His Way". We also discussed parts of the "Philokalia", some writings of Saint Seraphim of Sarov, and the Didache, teachings of the 12 Holy Apostles of Christ. You can read this book as a story for contemplation, or a daily workbook of prayer. May your spiritual journey be fruitful, and bring you ever closer to God!

An unworthy servant,

Father Raphael

PS - Do note that this book is purely for a prayerful life towards God. Any external resources provided or presented here, are to help the faithful in their Christian life.

Heart of a pilgrim

Do we carry an excessive burden in our hearts, or are we traveling light in the journey of life, in our pilgrimage to find God and rest in Him?

Dear beloved,

I was very moved by the opening paragraph of the book "The Way of a Pilgrim", with the excitement of a child and the tears of a penitent. The unknown Russian pilgrim confessed his faith in the grace of God, and his sins before God. He had nothing on him, except a backpack with some dried bread and a Holy Bible in his pocket.

When we walk the journey of life, what do we carry with us?

Do we shoulder the burden of many things and cling on to worldly possessions, or are we utilitarian in material needs but are voracious in our desire for growing towards God?

The pilgrim contemplated on Saint Paul's admonition (1 Thessalonians 5:17, and Ephesians 6:18) on "praying unceasingly". That became the reason and motivation for him to travel as a pilgrim, in search of answers. And like the pilgrim, we are too, pilgrims in life, in search of meaning, in search of life, in search of God. And I am convinced that Saint Paul's words pointed us directly to just what we need for meaning, life and God. But how?

Every morning, as we observe and pray the daily rule, for a brief moment in time, and a window of our lives, we focus on our attention towards God. But yet, as many of us lead lives in the world, we become hurried and hassled in the daily grind, and between those tasks we have to do, sometimes just to survive, we lost track of God. How then, as the pilgrim asked, can we attain this unceasing prayer?

The pilgrim went to various monasteries, in search of answers, and yet, he found none. At every place, when kindly abbots would offer him shelter and food, the pilgrim's singular attention was not on material comforts, but a focused attention on just wanting the answers to attaining unceasing prayer. I often lament when I revisit the pages of the book that I am but weak and frail in spirit and body, and do not have the resolve of this pilgrim, who, as we read in later pages, has a physical disability. I can only say I am unworthy in many ways, compared to this godly pilgrim, whose journey inspires me.

I am often encouraged by the words of Saint Macarius the Great, our father among the saints, who said: "One must force himself to prayer when he has not spiritual prayer; and thus God, beholding him thus striving and compelling himself by force, in spite of an unwilling heart, gives him the true prayer of the Spirit."

Saint Macarius' words exactly echoed the words of a starets who advised the pilgrim, that the inner desire to find unceasing prayer, is itself a grace from God, and a calling from God. One must relinquish his personal will, to allow God's grace to call out to us, to return to Him in inner prayer. The starets also advised, that while many teachers have written much on prayer, many do not realize that prayer is like breathing - it must unite with the rhythm of life. It should not be a mechanistic or methodical procedure, but truly to live and breathe the inner prayer. The starets reminded us of Saint Isaac the Syrian, who likewise said that the discipline of prayer is the root of all spiritual blessings ("Acquire the mother and she will bear you children.")

Let us pray, beloved, the prayer of the heart (from the Philokalia):

> *"Lord Jesus Christ, Son of God,*
> *have mercy on me, a sinner."*

Quiet places & spiritual direction

To find true inner prayer, are we willing to give up our material needs, find a good teacher and a quiet spot?

Dear beloved,

Let us continue the journey through the book "The Way of a Pilgrim".

The starets advised the pilgrim of the importance of a spiritual director and his guidance (Jeremiah 10:23), for one to lead a good inner prayerful life. Likewise, in our spiritual pilgrimage, let us pray to God, and ask for His infinite mercy and grace, to grant us a good spiritual director, or directors, in various phases of our journey in life. Do not be surprised, that every phase in our lives, God may grant us different spiritual directors. God's mysteries are sometimes impossible to understand rationally, but let Him take charge in our lives.

The starets explained to the pilgrim the advice of Saint Simeon the New Theologian, which one should sit in a quiet place alone (St Matthew 6:6), bowing the head and closing the eyes. Then breathe slowly, and slowly bring all of one's thoughts into the heart, striving to allow the thoughts to cede, and pray either softly or in the mind, "Lord Jesus Christ, Son of God, have mercy on me, a sinner."

Sometimes, when we pray, our minds begin to wander and drift off with unending and distracting thoughts. The pilgrim experienced the same. The devil is extremely disturbed at a prayerful person, and will stop at nothing to distract you away from prayer, since prayer leads you back to God.

What is interesting to note, is that the starets explained that when we are not humble, our own selves will empower and embolden the devil to be able to distract us. Nothing defeats the devil more easily, than a humble person in deep focused prayer, especially that of the confessional prayer of the heart with reverence and frequency, "Lord Jesus Christ, Son of God, have mercy on me, a sinner."

The pilgrim, under the guidance of the starets, started slowly with 3,000 prayers of the heart per day, to 6,000 per day, slowly and steadily, without rushing through each prayer. And soon, the pilgrim felt inner joy when he prayed unceasingly and longed for prayerful solitude, away from people and distractions. Eventually, the pilgrim managed 12,000 prayers per day. And not surprisingly, the more the pilgrim prayed, the more delighted and yearning he had to pray. God gave His mercy and grace on the pilgrim, one who sought only prayed to our Savior the Christ.

I have humbly found that in a hurried secular life, there is nothing more profoundly simple and yet edifying, than to seek to pray the prayer of the heart, for it is simple enough for anyone, no matter how busy, to pray between cracks of time between difficult and busy periods in a typical day.

After a delightful time with the starets, the pilgrim was again challenged spiritually, when the kind spiritual director died. The pilgrim once again was alone. In the transient life journey we go through, we are often presented with many of the same instances of fleeting moments, such as death itself. The pilgrim sought solace in the prayer of the heart. And strangely, the more he prayed, the more good he saw in people he met. Often, we come across people who may present challenges to our persons, and even cause us to lose our spirituality. But the pilgrim has shown us that by always returning to the prayer of the heart, we will perhaps lose sight of the negativity in the traits and behavior of people we come in contact with, and begin to see the good in them. Let us find an image of Christ in everyone we meet, and let us return to inner prayer always, whenever we find difficulty, or perhaps when we find negativity in people, for it is us who have sinned when we view others negatively.

The pilgrim eventually spent his only money on an old copy of the Philokalia, his very own, which he found to be the greatest treasure other than the Holy Bible he carried in his pocket. He has shown us that there is no greater treasure than Holy Scripture, and that wealth is nothing unless we spend it wisely. Are we carrying our wealth like shackles and chains, or are we using it like the tools of grace?

Let us keep the prayer of the heart often, deep in our heart:

> *"Lord Jesus Christ, Son of God,
> have mercy on me, a sinner."*

Prayer in distracting life moments

How often do we bring prayer into the center of our lives, to internalize it as a heartbeat or our breathing?

Dear beloved,

After the pilgrim managed to get a very old copy of the Philokalia, he was overjoyed. Together with the Holy Bible, and dried bread bits given by kindhearted souls, he set off his journey again.

This reminds me of a time that, despite my scoliosis, I traveled and walked a long distance in Japan, and the journey took its toll on me then, and for later years.

The pilgrim too, traveled, and for far greater distances. But unlike the sinner like me, he prayed the Jesus Prayer unceasingly, and he was not exhausted (1 Thessalonians 5:17, and Ephesians 6:18). The Jesus Prayer alone filled his thoughts and nothing else could distract him, not the pain of walking miles and miles on end, not the cold bitter weather, because the warmth of inner prayer filled his soul. Even if he fell sick, the prayed took the pains and suffering away. The pilgrim became immune to the ambient and environmental conditions, which became nothing more than noise in the background. The pilgrim's ego was increasingly given away to a complete utter foolishness for Christ, without pride or prejudice. The world might have thought of the pilgrim as nothing but a fool, but God's mercy gave the pilgrim something all of us would yearn for, an inner peace and complete joy in the love and warmth of God, through the Jesus Prayer.

Now the part of the story revealed that our pilgrim has a disability in his left arm since childhood, which prevented him from getting any suitable work or getting money for lodging. In him we could not find signs of despair nor resignation, but one of acceptance. Too often, sometimes we give way to our suffering, however small, and sometimes some of us might even blame God for our suffering (Ecclesiastes 7:14). God has been there before we even came about, and He knew us before we exist or imagine we know ourselves. I am often consoled that in apparent suffering, when I am wavering on my frail faith, I would return to prayer and somehow, God's mercy would lend strength for me to brave on. God would not want us to be perpetual babies, but to grow and mature in faith and love towards God. Every day is a day of grace and mercy to walk to Him, a baby step at a time (LXX Psalm 26:14).

The pilgrim, on following the disciplined verbal prayer of the heart, began to slowly find the prayer moved from merely from the lips, to be from the heart (Proverbs 28:19). The pilgrim described it as if the prayer would resonate with natural breathing patterns. Often, when we pray the Jesus Prayer in between busy moments in life, and in crowded places, it may be turned inwards into the heart, a soft and gentle resonance within our hearts, virtually unknown to people around us. Every little distraction, whether it be a colleague asking us for something, an office email to finish, a report to compile, some documents to photocopy at the photocopier, or even making a cup of tea for the afternoon, can be a prayerful moment to spend with the precious Jesus Prayer, deep within our heart, silently, without verbalizing. It can be a rejuvenating and calming prayer.

The pilgrim described, at this stage, the prayer has formed a "delicate soreness" in his heart, which brought an immense love for Jesus Christ.

He described that he would gladly throw himself at Christ's feet, embrace His holy feet and never let them go, with tears of joy and gratefulness for His mercy. The question perhaps is, do we pray for mere deliverance and material fulfillments, or would we rather pray for such tenderness and gratefulness of our faith and love for Christ?

The pilgrim gave us also, a wise reminder. He revisited the Philokalia, to pore over the text of the fathers, to discern the "delicate soreness" he felt, to be sure of what he was feeling was neither a delusion nor a mistake. Too often, we hear of believers (or even pre-believers) who fall prey to the lures of the devil, whose trickery can convince many of the signs and wonders. Let us therefore, follow the footpath of the saints before us, who sought only God and His mercy upon their sins, and not focus on signs and wonders. If we are praying, the devil will attempt to thwart us with laziness, sleepiness, and sometimes, what seem like miraculous signs. However, if we were to discern and revisit the holy texts, we would begin to see, what the fruits of the signs are. The devil does not lead us to God. This means that the devil's illusory signs to trick us can be easily rejected if we let our egos go, and allow God's will to take over. If however, we allow our pride to take over, then we will ignore and turn blind to the narrow path God has carved out painstakingly for us. The beauty of the Jesus Prayer therefore, is in its seeming simplicity. There are no esoteric sounds or lengthy discourses, just a short confessional prayer to profess our faith in Christ our Lord, and in the same prayer, lies a deeper and richer power - the name of God.

"Win the enemies in your mind with the name of God. You will not find any other weapon more effective than this. Similarly you will manage both to appease your passions inside yourself and to efface them with the aid of the prayer," said Saint John Climacus, father among the saints who wrote the illuminating "Ladder of Divine Ascent".

Let us try to bring our prayer from our lips, into our heart:

> *"Lord Jesus Christ, Son of God,*
> *have mercy on me, a sinner."*

Consolations during adversity

During our moments of despair and desolation, what is our heart saying? Are we closer to God, or further away?

Dear beloved,

In life, especially many of us who are truly in the world, laboring away to make a simple living for us, and our precious families, facing adversity is part of what we experience. For many of us, it is laboring away to make a simple living to take care of our beloved families. For others, we have to be caregivers of relatives who have become chronically ill, with medical and other expenses to think about. There seem to be many possible permutations to what adversity takes shape to snarl at us in our faces. What then, do we do in the face of adversity?

As our pilgrim progresses in his prayer and his reading of the Philokalia, he began to understand the writings of the fathers in the holy text more. The pilgrim has shown us that prayer must precede study, because our limited persons cannot possibly understand the deeper teachings of Christ. Only through a sustained faithful prayer over a length of time (Nehemiah 9), and certainly not a timeframe we determine, but God's timeframe, asking for His mercy to open our eyes, before we begin to be able to unravel the mysteries and beauty of the many sacred texts of the fathers. The pilgrim also explained that sometimes, the reposed starets would appear in his dreams, to explain parts of the Philokalia to him. And the pilgrim would read and pray in the day, and walked only at night, to make best use of the light of the day. Wherever he went, he asked only for dried bread and some salt for sustenance, and would then walked on again. The pilgrim demonstrated to us a constancy of prayer, a disciplined and ascetic approach to daily life, with little attachment to the material world.

However, his blissful prayerful state was soon disrupted, when he was hit unconscious by two soldiers, and robbed of his only possessions - the knapsack containing his Holy Bible and the Philokalia.

From a blissful and tender state, the pilgrim was reduced to deep grief with tears day and night. He lost his Holy Bible, which has comforted him in his childhood, his most intimate possession, and his copy of the Philokalia, his most recent treasure that has brought him closer to God. He wished for death rather than to live (Jonah 4). That was when the starets appeared to the pilgrim once again, and told the pilgrim that the incident was one of Divine mercy and grace, to prevent the pilgrim from sinking into attachment of material possessions and spiritual greed. Sometimes, in our pilgrimage, we look for spiritual consolations, and focus on them, rather than focusing on God Himself. We become greedy, possessed by our own inner demons and our own will, rather than sinking into the deep oasis of God's will. The starets in the dream, explained to the pilgrim that sometimes, we have to grieve before we can find closeness to God once again (1 Corinthians 10:13). Imagine this. If we are given a life of luxury and comfort with no trouble at all throughout life, how will we ever understand how much we have been blessed with? How can we learn of true love for those endowed with less, unless God shows us how wretched we truly are?

The pilgrim woke from the dream relieved, and picked himself up, and started praying the Jesus Prayer with the Sign of the Cross once again, and asked God's will be done. In returning to the basics of humility and constancy of prayer, he found the heart of peace again.

Life is never a constant. It is transient. God revealed His mercy upon the pilgrim once again, when the pilgrim's path converged with a convoy of convicts, among them the two soldiers who robbed him earlier. He pleaded with the two soldiers and offered to pay them a small fee if he could have his Holy Bible and the Philokalia back.

The pilgrim found his Holy Bible and the Philokalia, in the care of the Captain who supervised the transit of the convoy. The Captain was a religious man who then shared a meal with the pilgrim.

The Captain revealed that in his youth, he was taken to alcoholism and that destroyed his life. The Captain eventually met a monk who instructed him to read the Bible every time his urge for the bottle returned. At first, the Captain could not understand the Bible at all. However, even as reluctant and unrepentant he was, God's mercy permeates through any person who would bother to open up the Holy Bible, and His grace would reform any person. Eventually, truly, by the mercy of God, the Captain's inner demons were banished by his slow and steady embrace of the reading of the Bible. Every time his urge for the bottle returned, he braved on to read yet another chapter of the Holy Bible. The monk told the Captain that Saint John Chrysostom, father among the saints, said that the very presence of the Holy Bible would chase evil spirits away. The Captain eventually reformed, regained his rank and status, and kept close to his breast pocket, a Holy Bible everywhere he went and prayed.

At this juncture, the Captain asked the pilgrim whether the Jesus Prayer or the Holy Bible is more exalted. The pilgrim said that to him, both are the same, because the most holy name of Jesus Christ contained the entire truth of the Bible, and that the holy Fathers said that the Jesus Prayer is the abbreviated form of the entire Bible. This is the mystery of the Jesus Prayer, a mercy and grace from God, through the holy name of Jesus Christ our Lord (St John 14:13-14).

Dear beloved, let us pray,

> *"Lord Jesus Christ, Son of God,*
> *have mercy on me, a sinner."*

Physical, mental & heart activities

When we flip open the Holy Bible and writings, do we feel drawn to them with reverence, awe and love?

Dear beloved,

The pilgrim prayed with the good captain the previous night. When he woke up, he immediately went back to reading the Philokalia again. The pilgrim described the feeling as one of immense joy, as if he was reunited with a father he loved a great deal. The pilgrim therefore, is like an honest mirror. When we read the Holy Scripture and writings, do we feel drawn to them with love and joy? Do we show not just love, but reverence as well?

One part the Philokalia, written by Saint Theophilus of Philadelphia, explained that humans can perform 3 separate activities simultaneously, namely: (1) eat, (2) read, and (3) pray. Let us break these activities down. Eating is a "physical" activity, one that sustains us. It need not be something we indulge incessantly. Reading is a "mental" activity, one that allows us read the

Holy texts to awaken a part of us spiritually. And prayer, the most important activity of all, is an activity "from the heart", and should be the heartbeat and breathing that allows our reading to take on new meaning, growing closer to God every moment. As we pray, think about the needs of others, and the wretched state we are in and the immense mercy God has given us in many life's circumstances. Therefore, we can consider what activities in our lives are physical and mental, and give a sacred space to the activity of the heart - prayer.

The pilgrim parted company with the captain, and the captain kindly gave a little money to the pilgrim. The pilgrim remembered his promise to the two soldiers who robbed him, that he would pay them. He kept his promise to them and gave the little money the captain gave him, to the soldiers (Romans 12:20, St Matthew 5:44). In my own humble journey, Christ fully revealed His mercy to me, when I forgave someone who harmed me a great deal. When I had hatred or depression, I was blind to God's presence right next to me. But when I dropped my burden of hatred and depression, the love of Christ blossomed and I was able, through our God's mercy on an unworthy person like me, to receive Him, and to eventually become His servant.

The pilgrim kept walking, braving on in his journey. He kept praying, and kept referring back to the Philokalia. The only grief the pilgrim talked about was that he hoped he could find a permanent space to read the Philokalia and Holy Bible in peace. The pilgrim began to realize what the Holy Fathers meant when they said that the Philokalia is like the key to unlock the hidden meanings of the Holy Bible, because the pilgrim began to make more and more progress by reading both the Philokalia and the Holy Bible, strengthened by constant prayer.

Eventually, the pilgrim met a forester who lived deep in the forest, and lamented to the forester that he led such a wonderfully blessed eremitic life. The pilgrim has always shown to us, a heart of a hermit. Many of us however, are not hermits. We are called to be part of the world, to be in the world with others. If so, why would we want to be eremitic, or to have the heart of a hermit? The answer lies in inner prayer. When we go into our spiritual closet and pray, we are much like the hermits who left communities of people, to wander into the desert, where you find no one, see nothing but sand on end, and the plain deep blue sky. When we go about the daily routine, working, caring, eating, walking, we can still go into our spiritual closet and pray, with the heart safely secured in prayer, even as we engage in physical and mental activities.

The forester offered to the pilgrim a tremendous opportunity - to be with him in the forest, without any other human intervention, until the autumn when nearby people come forward to fell the trees. So the pilgrim gladly accepted to live off the land in the forest, knowing full well how transient this blessing would be, lasting until the autumn. Likewise, in life, we will face many opportunities and challenges. Each of these events will be transient, good or bad. Too often, we may cling on to particular events, people or places, and forget that all things must pass, because everything is part of God's will, as well as His mercy that we may not fully understand. The pilgrim, unlike many, gladly accepted the offer to stay in the forest, and saw that as a great joy. How often do we take whatever that comes our way, however little it appear to our myopic eyes, that it may represent a great blessing, however transient? Have we examined these events in life and realized that they are not mere coincidences or mundane occurrences, but represent the greater reasons of God? Are we blissfully content with our lives and live them out walking in the ways of Christ (1 Timothy 6:6, and Hebrews 13:5)?

Would you consider walking with me, spending today, to pray the prayer of the heart, in between the cracks of time whenever you can?

> *"Lord Jesus Christ, Son of God,*
> *have mercy on me, a sinner."*

Simple prayers & redemption

When we look to God, are we going to Him
out of fear, or out of greed? Or do we
approach Him with just a simple love?

Dear beloved,

The pilgrim settled in the forest with the forester, as caretakers for the forest. The forester recounted his story to the pilgrim. He was a successful businessman who sinned a great deal. Eventually, he met an old deacon who read him the Book of Revelation. After learning about the suffering of the sinners at Christ's return, the man gave up his business and took up the job as a forester, in exchange for simple bread, clothes, and candles for prayers.

The forester spent the next ten years in the forest, following a strict prayer rule every day, with the life of a monastic. For ten years, the forester found great peace and joy (Romans 5).

But the forester explained to the pilgrim that lately, he began to experience a loss of faith, questioning the truth in the Word of God, and even wondered if he should pack up and return to being a businessman instead.

One of the worst thoughts the evil one can do to us is to instill a sense of hopelessness and doubt. With doubt comes loss of faith, and eventually, a sad apathy that denounces the existence of God and His Word. The pilgrim considered that the devil does not segregate between the rich or the poor; but will attack anyone with even a shred of faith in God, and he will attack more ferociously if a person has steadfast faith in God, seeking to destroy such a man completely. Know this, the devil is void of love, and knows only hatred, for he was cast out of Heaven and is stricken with an eternal hatred for the loved creation of God - mankind.

The pilgrim was sympathetic to the forester, and read Saint Hesychios' admonitions in the Philokalia to him. Accordingly, the pilgrim explained that some people might abstain from sin out of the fear of eternal suffering, while some others might desire the fruit of Heaven out of greed. Both kinds of people would not find God, and would fall prey to the fruits of the evil one, because they try to find God with the heart of slaves, or hearts of mercenaries. God desires that we return to Him as sons, out of pure love and simple devotion. The pilgrim shared with the forester, the power of the name of Christ, through the prayer of the heart (Philippians 4:13).

In many of our own spiritual journeys, we might seek esoteric materials, and may get sidetracked on our singular and narrow journey seeking God and His face. While all these time, God only wanted us to return to Him, and to shine the light of true love back to Him, just as He has been so lovingly shining His light of love, grace and mercy, continuously on us. We may be blind to His light for so long, but He was there, still is there, and will always be there.

The pilgrim gave spiritual rest to the forester, and then quickly retreated to his own cave, and started reading his Philokalia again. He was eager and determined, and read the book from the beginning to the end (1 Corinthians 12:31 and 1 Thessalonians 5:19). He started praying continuously to petition the Lord to grant him the mercy of knowing what the holy fathers wrote in the Philokalia, and eventually, he fell asleep. In his dream, his departed starets explained to him, that the Philokalia (like the Holy Bible) is a holy mystery, and would present simple wisdom to the simple, and deep wisdom to the wise.

The starets explained that the pilgrim, being a simple man, would benefit much more by NOT reading the Philokalia from the beginning to the end, but rather, in the order of (1) Saint Nicephorus the hermit, (2) Saint Gregory of Sinai, without the short chapters, (3) Saint Symeon the New Theologian, (4) Saint Callistus, (5) Saint Ignatius, and lastly, (6) summary on methods of prayer by Saint Callistus, which in this pattern, according to the departed starets, contained the necessary to understand the inner prayer of the heart for anybody. We will briefly discuss readings of Saint Nicephorus the hermit, Saint Gregory of Sinai, and Saint Symeon the New Theologian.

The pilgrim woke up at dawn, wondering if the departed starets did indeed appear to him or it might have been just a delusional thought in his own mind. He looked at his Philokalia which was on a rock table, and miraculously, the Philokalia was flipped to the exact page where the Starets mentioned, on methods of prayer by Saint Callistus, with charcoal markings as well! The pilgrim had lovingly wrapped his Philokalia and kept under his bed the previous night.

The pilgrim gave us a wise warning, that when one is eager and earnest about inner prayer, we must discern and pray unto God, so that we do not fall prey to delusions (1 John 4:1, St Matthew 24:24). When we pray, are we are simply praying and exalting God? Inner prayer is about reaching out to God, without ego, pride, greed, or malice. The closer we approach God with a pristine mind without the shackles of the primary sins, especially that of pride and greed, the more we can discern if we are indeed closer to God, or closer to the evil one. How so?

Imagine approaching inner prayer with an intention of wanting to be "better" than someone else. The evil one will sense your pride and greed, and present you with signs and wonders, deluding you that you have attained the inner prayer, when in fact you are nowhere near it. Praying must have a clear and honest intention, that of simply loving God and recognizing how far we are removed from His presence. The praying heart should not have any other motive of want - it should not have any beastly lust after prideful gains. This is an important consideration when approaching inner prayer. The devil will often trick us with what we want to see through our own passions, while God will only show us what IS - the Truth. We will read through the book more on this next.

I often find the greatest consolation when praying, to simply forget the daily worries for a while, and focus only on God. I simply pray the Jesus prayer, dropping my emotional burdens, my work challenges, my pretensions, my pride, my worries, my passions, and simply pray silently in my heart - the Jesus prayer. I do not ask God of anything, and when distractions arise, I return to the Jesus prayer. Even if I must engage in conversation at work, my heart is never far from the Jesus prayer. There is a simple beauty of the Jesus prayer, which also infers the truth of the love of God - He does not leave any of us behind, even as He knows how far we have fallen behind. Let us pray:

> *"Lord Jesus Christ, Son of God,*
> *have mercy on me, a sinner."*

Lessons: St Nicephorus the Hermit

We learn the guarding of our heart, and the basics of the Jesus Prayer from Saint Nicephorus the Hermit from the Philokalia.

Dear beloved,

We will attempt to go through the Philokalia as the reposed starets taught the pilgrim in a dream. Let us go according to the instruction of the starets, by starting with the teaching of Saint Nicephorus the Hermit from Mount Athos, concerning sobriety and the guarding of the heart.

Saint Nicephorus first mentioned that finding eternal life by finding the Kingdom of God within us (Luke 17:21) is a science, and even more of an art. This means that in the Orthodox tradition, importance is given more to an experience from the heart, than simply rational and logical deductions through the mind more commonly associated with Western traditions. When we walk towards God, it is not merely a mechanistic deduction to knowing about God, and then finding scientific means to attaining spirituality.

Rather, in the Orthodox tradition, we are looking at an experience, that of finding God's love (2 Timothy 2:13), and returning as much love as we can summon, to God. When we love someone, we tend to desire to give as much as we possess to that person. And if we truly love someone unconditionally, we would desire to give as much as we possess to that person, without qualification, without hesitation, without caution (Proverbs 17:17).

Saint Nicephorus advised that we should first return to our inner selves, before we can attempt to be reconciled back with God. What does that mean? All too often, we seek external methods that are alien and unrealistic to our inner nature, and try to harshly "marry" those methods to our hearts desiring God. In the end, all we can find will be barren deserts lacking in any closeness to God and His dew of love. Imagine ourselves as a child, who has consistently neglected the home we have, the loving parents we have, and we go out often to look for company and fun (Luke 15:11-32). While those we meet outside may be fun sometimes, there will always be competition, lack of authenticity, and lack of emotional depth. Only when we drop our playfulness and return home to the arms of our loving parents, do we begin to find the true love, the comfort, the peace, and contentment. It is the same as seeking the Kingdom of God - that of returning to our inner selves.

Saint Nicephorus quoted Saint John of the Ladder, to equate our spirituality like a house, which is frequently besieged by thieves and robbers, for the treasure of the heart within. Saint John of the Ladder, as well as Saint Macarius the Great, advised us that we should guard our bodies, our tongues, and our hearts. When we are vigilant and constantly in prayer, especially calling on the name of Jesus Christ our Lord, we can detect and resist the attacks of the devil against our hearts (1 Peter 5:8). Saint Isaac of Syria also described that the ladder to the Kingdom of God is hidden within us, consistent with all the great fathers among the saints, who reminded us, time and again, to guard our hearts and manifested actions, like a treasure house worthy of protection and nurture.

Saint John of Karpathos added that when we pray, it should not be cavalier and occasional, but consistent, disciplined, much like how we would labor for our food and living at our jobs, because we are afraid to be unemployed. Likewise, would we not see our salvation as even more important than a mere job, and labor so much more for it?

Every second, our mind drifts through thoughts, which may drift off to nothingness, or be nurtured into actions. Saint Symeon the New Theologian reminded us that the devil would thwart our prayerful lives by injecting new distracting ideas into us, or to fester what our sinful nature already imagined (2 Corinthians 2:11). Saint Symeon said that the only way against the devil's constant battles against our souls is to have a constant remembrance of God. In every breath, every step, every gesture, every word, every action, let us attempt to keep a remembrance of our God, so that all these visible actions may be transfigured into faith and love by the mercy of God.

Next, Saint Nicephorus taught us, beginners, how to pray the Jesus prayer.

He asked us to breath in, and draw the air with our mind, to enter our heart, and attempt to keep our mind within our heart, with the prayer "Lord Jesus Christ, Son of God, have mercy on me, a sinner". Whenever the mind drifts away with thoughts, positive or negative, return it with the breath, into the heart. Breathe in and out naturally with the flow of the prayer within our heart. By praying silently, we are bringing the prayer into our hearts. It should not be a painful and fidgety experience, as we are NOT trying to restrain the mind, but to allow it to sense the joy of the Jesus Prayer resting and resonating with the heart (1 Thessalonians 5:16-18). In the beginning, it will be difficult, as much as I find it difficult to explain the exact feeling. But the more, and the longer you rest the Jesus Prayer frequently within your heart by drawing in your mind, the more peace you will find.

We will continue with the teachings of Saint Gregory of Sinai tomorrow, from the Philokalia concerning the inner prayer.

"Lord Jesus Christ, Son of God, have mercy on me, a sinner".

Lessons: St Gregory of Sinai

Have we become Christians only in name?
Saint Gregory of Sinai teaches us how to
be active and living in Christ.

Dear beloved,

For some, Holy Baptism becomes the beginning, and the end, a mere "badge" of a Christian living without walking in the ways of Christ. In the Philokalia, Saint Gregory of Sinai gave us his thoughts on how to avoid being such a Christian, but to act and live according to how Christ have commanded, and how He lived.

Saint Gregory mentioned that after our Holy Baptism and Chrismation, we should maintain a conversation with our Lord Jesus Christ. What is this conversation? Is it simply asking for favors from God? No. Saint Gregory mentioned this conversation as the pure prayer of the heart. What is pure prayer of the heart? It is a simple heart with no desire other than loving God, without expecting anything from God, but pleading simply for His mercy.

We should also, according to Saint Gregory,

keep the laws of God diligently (St Matthew 4:17). Keeping the laws of God should not be a carnal passion of self-torture. It should be a joyous keeping of His laws because it will open our eyes and hearts to sensing His gifts to us better and better, and to be closer and closer to Him. God is purity, and in our defiled state it is impossible for us to draw near to Him, much less be near Him. Therefore, the more we keep to His laws with a pure and joyous heart, the closer we can walk to Him without getting blown away by His sheer brilliance and power.

Saint Gregory mentioned that on top of keeping God's laws, the second, and more powerful method, is to invoke unceasingly, the name of Jesus Christ our Lord. The more we attend to prayer, the more the prayer displaces our passions, akin to filling up our cup with vintage wine of God's salvation, than the filth from the drains due to our passions. The prayer, when prayed with a pure heart, also calls on the comfort of the Holy Spirit, which helps us draw our active mind into the heart, and stills it. Saint Gregory mentioned that the more we pray the Jesus Prayer, the more the prayer will warm and ignite our hearts to love our Lord even more.

Next, Saint Gregory gave recommendations to praying the Jesus Prayer. He recommended a very low stool to sit on, and breathing naturally to aid our easily distracted mind, and say, "Lord Jesus Christ, Son of God, have mercy on me, a sinner". Saint Gregory also mentioned that when thoughts arise, we are to ignore them whether they are good and bad.

This in itself is both an encouragement for us to tend to praying the Jesus Prayer, as well as a description of what the fruits of pure and orthodox prayer should be - that of growing a pure and simple love for our Lord. Do not be persuaded by any other sign other than a pure heart of loving our Lord. Even if signs should arise, return to the prayer of the heart.

But, alas, we are no saints, and we are easily distracted by aches from sitting on the stool for too long (or even a short while). Saint Gregory asked us then, if pains and distractions become too much, to stand up and chant the Psalms or a passage from the Holy Bible, or even tend to an uncommon chore or work. However, Saint Gregory warned us against reading books in conflict with the inner prayer, because our minds are active and will be distracted. For example, if we are praying the Jesus Prayer, we may not want to read complex books related to our profession or trade, or distracting magazines on secular and material issues.

Saint Gregory asked us not to abandon prayer books. Some people might imagine just praying the Jesus Prayer is sufficient. No extreme is good. Everything should be done in moderation. Saint Gregory mentioned prayer books, the Holy Bible and writings of the Holy Fathers, as means to strengthen us during moments of weakness.

A very important thing Saint Gregory warned us to guard against is "prelest", or spiritual deception of the evil one (Revelation 12:9). As we have frequently read or heard before, the devil is full of deceit and hatred. The closer we attempt to draw near to God, the harsher and more determined he will be to destroy us and our nascent faith. How does prelest arise? It is when we attempt to pray beyond our capabilities, and even beyond what grace and mercy we deserve, the devil may present spiritual signs to us to trick us into believing we are at that special place of the inner prayer of the heart. Often, it is far from it. Therefore, the Jesus Prayer serves two great purposes, (1) calling on the miraculous power and infinite strength of Jesus Christ our Lord and Redeemer, and (2) more importantly, confessing our terribly fallen state as a sinner. Nothing weakens the devil more than our pure and true confession of our sins (2 Ezra 10). Saint Gregory calls this state "joyful sorrow", because we have found the joy of the Lord through invoking His name and bringing our mind into our heart, and we are sorrowful because we recognize our fallen condition. But, our Lord gave us solace and comfort, and told us to have courage, because He is with us all of the days.

I find praying the Jesus Prayer a great comfort throughout the day in between moments of time: At work, during meals, walking, in a vehicle, in the washroom, almost anywhere where I can turn inwards (even during a boring meeting). And I keep praying the Daily Rule, and tend to other prayers as much as I can as a servant still in the world. Let us pray:

> *"Lord Jesus Christ, Son of God,*
> *have mercy on me, a sinner"*

What did Saint Symeon the New Theologian mean by praying in the Face of God to achieve freedom of all cares and passions?

Dear beloved,

Saint Symeon the New Theologian taught us about a prayer of purity, that only very few could attain. To the saint, only if our minds are free from everything, can we have the heart to examine the lures of the evil one, and then to repel these illusory temptations.

To put it in perspective, if we are praying and our heart wanders into thinking what God might grant us in terms of spiritual capabilities, the devil seizes this impure thought, and presents us with the possibilities of a deceptive "attainment". And if we are praying the Jesus Prayer and our mind begins to sink into the passions of the material world, the devil also senses that and quickly presents us with the deception that if we pray to God, our material needs will be fulfilled; when in fact, it will be the devil who will

48

transplant God's presence due to our own passions, and begin to seduce us to simply sinking into material passions. Imagine if we are to die this minute and meet God's Face, would our thoughts be pure from sin, our love only upon God and His creation? Or are our minds defiled with lots of distracting thoughts of passions that has no place in front of God?

Therefore, Saint Symeon was very clear, our minds must be free from ALL thoughts, other than the simple devoted prayer of the heart, so that our mind can guard our hearts, and we will receive the grace and mercy of God, to be able to discern, and act against the deception of the devil (St Matthew 17:4).

Often, when we visit a neighborhood food center, we have to be lenient when ordering and eating food there. This is because all too frequent, the utensils and plates are not clean. However, the economy and convenience of eating at these places far outweigh the labor of cooking our own, or the price tags of more expensive (and sometimes cleaner) environments. Therefore, it is the same with us. We not only clean ourselves on the outside, to look presentable to others, but we should also tend to our hearts through our minds, to keep our hearts loving and pure (St Matthew 23:26).

Saint Symeon mentioned 3 important things: (1) freedom from all cares, (2) a clear conscience, and (3) total dispassion.

What is freedom from all cares? This is a pristine state of condition that we are free from caring for the good and the bad, or what the Fathers called, "dead to all things". This means that while many of us would consider freeing our beings from bad things, we tend to gravitate to good things. Remember, the evil one is strong and cunning, and can take our passion for good things against us. If we have desire of good things, the devil will deceive us by drawing us closer and closer to the slavery of such "good things". Whether good or bad, many of us are stuck in this lack of freedom, because of our pride and vanity. If we examine all things without a sense of self-importance, we can quickly uncover that many things are simply a clinging on to our egos.

A clear conscience is difficult, for all of us are fallen, and we are constantly falling and getting up, falling and getting up. It is difficult for us, mere sinners, to stay in that pristine state of clear conscience. And yet, if we imagine what we do as building-sized billboards, then our sins are also these super-sized billboards, seen by all, and especially by God. Can we afford to stand in the Face of God with large ugly billboards that advertise our impurities? Therefore, we are told by our Lord to be perfect as our Father is perfect (St Matthew 5:48). We are not arrogant enough to imagine we are saints, but it is a clear instruction to us to keep our eyes of the laws of God, out of love, and not just out of posterity or fear.

Total dispassion is challenging to us because we who are in the world, deep in it, are bombarded by many stimuli. And yet, Saint Symeon advised that only with total dispassion so that our mind does not regard or behold anything, can our heart be empty enough to be filled with the prayer of the heart towards God, and God can fill us with the tranquil love that is untainted by any other defiled things.

When we attempt to regulate our breathing and pray the prayer of the heart, we will frequently be met with inner conflict, temptations, distractions, and noise. Saint Symeon also mentioned that as we pray, we may find a certain hardness or darkness of our hearts, because the evil one will be hard at work to break our prayers down. We who pray are simple bricklayers, brick by brick do we build up our house of prayer. And the devil has a bulldozer or a big sledgehammer and is hell bent to breaking our humble attempts down. Therefore, Saint Symeon said we should keep on praying, until we find an unending joy, which is a pure love for our Lord. Remember, the evil one will cause "prelest" or spiritual deception to harm you always, and so you must discern what is true joy and love, from what is a cheap imitation. All the Fathers advised that one should always keep a spiritual director close, and abide by the advice of the spiritual director when attempting inner prayer.

Saint Symeon the New Theologian described the process of unceasing prayer as one of the Name of Jesus destroying any distracting or tempting thought that comes across, returning the heart and mind into the prayer again. So my beloved, let us pray:

"Lord Jesus Christ, Son of God,
have mercy on me, a sinner".

Efforts in prayer and inner joy

*Have we prayed long and hard enough
such that God opens up the heavens to
reveal His indescribable love to us?*

Dear beloved,

Let us return to our pilgrim in "The Way of a Pilgrim". The pilgrim followed the instructions of the starets in his vision, and soon, he began to experience a tender soreness in his heart, and after that, a sense of warmth, joy and peace. The more he prayed the prayer of the heart, the less concerned he became of other worldly issues. The sensations he felt varied from joy, freedom, grateful tears, and love for the Lord. No matter what the joyous and positive sensations were, the pilgrim experienced the Kingdom of God within him (St Luke 17:21).

The pilgrim described 3 effects of this inner prayer. First, he experienced a constant remembrance of God and loving Him in the spirit. Second, he experienced feelings of warmth and joy in the heart with little interest in sinning. Lastly, he experienced a gift of understanding

Holy Scripture better, even understanding how creatures communicate, dispassion for things in the world, and a firmer faith in the Lord. The pilgrim spent 5 months to pray, such that eventually, he was able to pray unceasingly in his heart, whether awake, or asleep. The pilgrim was able to multi-task, with an unceasing prayer in his heart, and yet tends to outward tasks such as listening to someone or reading.

Eventually, fall came and it was time for the pilgrim to leave. The pilgrim understood every condition in life to be a mercy and grace from God, and that everything from God is like a consolation, not to be an attachment to (Ecclesiastes 3:1-22). Therefore, he thanked the forester, kissed the ground that nourished him for months, and went on his way, contented. This is an important lesson for us in the world, that sometimes, when God grants us spiritual or material consolations, they are not meant for us to cling on to, or even lust after for more. They are meant as instruments of mercy during times of our weakness, and that we are to climb out of the pits and move on, strengthened and wiser (Daniel 2:21).

One day, a wolf attacked the pilgrim. A prayer

rope (chotki) given by the pilgrim's reposed starets saved him, when the prayer rope tangled the wolf's neck. The wolf struggled and the pilgrim bravely made a sign of the Cross, and tore the prayer rope off the wolf, and the wolf escaped. The pilgrim was unharmed.

Although people did not think the pilgrim was saved by Divine mercy, a teacher believed him. The teacher told the pilgrim that Adam was first created innocent and was able to control animals (Genesis 1:26-28). Saints always held a prayer rope in their hands and their holiness was entwined with their prayer ropes, much like the innocence of Adam. Therefore, the mystery of such holy innocence is why the Orthodox Church holds the relics of saints in high regard.

The pilgrim realized that the teacher was a wise man, and wanted to learn more about prayer from him. The teacher explained that all men are born to pray and exalt God, even if many did not realize that, sometimes even throughout life (Romans 8:20).

The pilgrim walked and walked, eventually reaching a small community. The local priest invited the pilgrim to stay, and to be a watchman over the construction workers building a new church in the community. The pilgrim reluctantly agreed, as long as he could read and pray. The pilgrim retreated to a chapel to read and pray, and soon, people in the community realized the faith of the pilgrim, and the pilgrim began to give his thoughts to the community folks. He even taught a young peasant girl how to pray the Jesus prayer. The young girl was so devoted and disciplined that soon, she too found the inner joy of praying the Jesus prayer.

Eventually, the villagers who came to him regularly to ask for advice overwhelmed the pilgrim. The pilgrim had the heart of a hermit and was very uncomfortable in tending to the queries and prayer needs of people. So eventually he bade the priest goodbye, and decided to leave. This is an important lesson for us. Some of us are ordained to be monks or solitaries, who will lead an austere life of discipline and unceasing intercessory prayer for the benefit of mankind. Some others will have an ordained secular family life, where they will be deep in the world, and bring out growing families. In our journey in life, we should try our best to be open to listening, and discern if indeed God has given us specific talents, or if some of us are destined for other things. But whether eremitic or secular, one thing stands out that unites all of us - prayer. Even if we find prayer difficult at times for many of us in the world, remember this saying from Saint Macarius the Great (Coptic):

"One must force himself to prayer when he has not spiritual prayer; and thus God, beholding him thus striving and compelling himself by force, in spite of an unwilling heart, gives him the true prayer of the Spirit."

Let us pray:

"Lord Jesus Christ, Son of God, have mercy on me, a sinner".

Steadfast faith against all odds

When assailed by the evil one, what state of mind do we have? Fear? Anger? Or an immovable faith and trust in God?

Dear beloved,

Some people find it hard to understand the meaning of monasticism. Conversely, for some of my friends in the pastoral labors (monastic or not), they would also find it difficult to understand many of the secular challenges we face in the world. But yet, each of us is ordained by God and equipped by Him with different gifts, to tend to different tasks, and to lead different lives. The unifying foundation for all of us is that God desires all of us to reconcile from our fallen state, back to Him.

Likewise, the pilgrim was talking to a priest who kept persuading him to labor with him in Church, but the pilgrim would not, but very much desired to continue his journey as a lonely pilgrim. Therefore, to the pilgrim, God has given him the blessing of a pilgrim who would lead a solitary life, dedicated to prayer.

Father among the saints, Saint John Chrysostom, said: "For even one dwelling in a city may imitate the self-denial of the monks; yes, one who has a wife, and is busy in a household, may pray, and fast, and learn compunction. Since they also, who at the first were instructed by the Apostles, though they dwelt in cities, yet showed forth the piety of the occupiers of the deserts: and others again who had to rule over workshops, as Priscilla and Aquila. (Homilies on Saint Matthew, number 55).

Soon after, the young girl who learned the Jesus Prayer from the pilgrim ran to him, pleading with him to take her with him. The young girl was to be betrothed to a schismatic, and she would not want to. Just when they were talking, people from the village caught up with her, and dragged her back to the village. The villagers chained the pilgrim and accused him of seducing the young girl. However, the village priest who employed the pilgrim for sometime, promised to stand testimony for him. And when the magistrate presided on the case, he determined that the young girl was to be handled by her parents, while the pilgrim would be caned and then thrown out of the village.

The pilgrim was not disturbed or angry (Ephesians 4:31-32), but praised God for allowing him to suffer for His name, and the pilgrim joyfully returned to unceasing prayer. The young girl's mother saw the pilgrim, told him that the person whom the girl was to be betrothed to, had severed the impending marriage. The mother gratefully gave him some bread.

Often, when the evil one assails us, some of us might be tempted to lapse into a fallen state, and become angry or even harbor hatred. The devil will then "fan the fires" and we will sink deeper and deeper in the abyss, and become a slave to the devil's labors (St James 1:20).

The starets again appeared to the pilgrim in a dream, to advise him the teaching of Saint John of Karpathos, where teachers are sometimes placed in situations of shame and temptations, so that others may benefit spiritually and gain the strength of faith. Even in the worst of challenges, we are to remember that Christ is above all creation and the evil one's works (1 John 4:4).

Our consolation is in the Lord, and His Divine mercy and grace on our failings. We are called to be marathon runners, to last throughout our lives, to persevere to the very end when we face death squarely. If we fall during many parts of our lives, we are to dust ourselves and pick ourselves up and start running towards God again (Proverbs 24:16).

The starets also instructed the pilgrim through the dream, that if one persists in prayer, he should record down everything, and teach the inner prayer to others. The Christian community is one of strengthening, edifying, and nurturing the faith of other Christians (Proverbs 18:19).

One day, the pilgrim felt an irresistible desire to receive Communion, on the feast day of the Annunciation of the Most Holy Theotokos. He found a church some distance away, and walked, and walked. He was totally drenched by a heavy rain, but managed to reach the church in time for the Holy Mystery in such an important feast day. The Mystery of the Communion is a beautiful event and should be treasured, celebrated as often as we can. It is the means of partaking in the wondrous joy, with fear and trembling as many of us experience on a frequent basis, awed by the Divine Liturgy and the prayers.

Because the rain, the pilgrim's legs became

infected and completely paralyzed, unable to walk. He was chased out of the compound and collapsed at the church steps and laid there for two days, totally ignored by people walking by when he pleaded for help.

When those who are suffering, and in pain, ask us for help, are we blind to their woes? Or do we tend to them as we see in them, an image of Christ? (St Matthew 25:35).

Let us pray unto our Lord, with the heart of a penitent:

> *"Lord Jesus Christ, Son of God,*
> *have mercy on me, a sinner".*

Divine mercy in the worst of times

*Do not despair even in the worst of times,
or the most painful suffering, for our God's
mercy will prevail.*

Dear beloved,

Remember our pilgrim? His legs were paralyzed and he collapsed in front of the church, ignored by many. A peasant came to him and said he could heal him, in exchange for something. The pilgrim lamented that he did not have anything valuable to give the peasant. The peasant then asked if the pilgrim would work for him for a season. The pilgrim said that he could not work due to a complete disability of one arm, but could read and write. The peasant gladly asked the pilgrim to teach his son to write, as tutors were expensive.

The peasant collected many rotting bones of animals and made tar out of the bones, and applied the liquid on the pilgrim's legs. In just five days, the pilgrim could walk around with a cane, and was healed completely in just one week! The pilgrim thanked God for His wondrous creation, that even a pile of rotting bones could bring life back to damaged limbs, surely an affirmation of the resurrection and life ever after (St Luke 18:27).

When the pilgrim recovered, he started teaching the peasant's boy, by using the Jesus Prayer. Eventually, a local estate steward saw the boy and was impressed enough to ask who his tutor was. The steward found the pilgrim and saw him reading the Philokalia. However, the steward was not impressed by the Philokalia and thought that the "endless repetition" of the Jesus Prayer was insane and not productive to the spiritual life.

The pilgrim corrected the heterodox mind of the steward, and mentioned that the Philokalia was written by some of the greatest Orthodox minds, including Saint Anthony the Great (Coptic), Saint Macarius the Great, Saint Mark the Anchorite, Saint John Chrysostom, and many others. The Philokalia contained the purest form of inner prayer, which inspired many other traditions that eventually corrupted the original teachings. Therefore, in all manner of inner prayer, there is nothing like the Philokalia, which preserved the truest inner prayer to God (St Mark 13:33). The pilgrim enlightened the steward that it was productive for a Christian to grow and mature in the faith, and not just adhere to the bare minimum of daily prayers or the occasional attendance at a Divine Liturgy. All too often, the pilgrim commented, that people grow lazy in the inner heart, and instead, focus just on superficial external works, and fall into pride, delusion, or isolation. The steward was impressed with the teachings of the Philokalia, and eventually, he invited the pilgrim over to his house and read the Philokalia to his wife and him.

One night, while the pilgrim was at the steward's house, the steward's wife choked on a fish bone. The reposed starets appeared to the pilgrim in his dream once again, and provided the unlikely cure of using lamp oil to extricate the fish bone from the steward's wife. When the pilgrim woke up, he immediately told the steward to use lamp oil, which caused the old lady to cough, and the fish bone came out. The steward could not believe the merciful miracle revealed to the pilgrim through a dream, and word soon got out to the community of the pilgrim's gifts (Jeremiah 30:17).

The pilgrim was afraid of falling into vainglory, and one night, slipped out of the community without informing anyone.

In our journey throughout life, there will be people who appreciate some of our humble gifts and talents. For example, we may be a good craftsman, healer, engineer, tailor, and so on. People may come to us frequently for advice or help, growing reliant on us, and sometimes, heaping flattering words onto us. Not everyone is a saint, and so sometimes, we lapse into prideful sin when we begin to indulge in these flattering words and may even begin to believe them to be true. That's a clear space for the evil one to tempt us further, to draw us away from our journey to God, and to keep us foolishly contented in an endless loop of suffering disguised as "joy". Therefore, the pilgrim was under the mercy of God, to discern such spiritual dangers, and left without any attachment (Galatians 5:26).

The pilgrim walked and walked, rejoicing at the great inner joy he got from inner prayer. There were stretches of paths he took where he felt as if he was the only person on earth. To many of us living deep in the world, this feeling is alien to us. We face many people every day, taking the bus, the transit train, getting a quick bite at the nearby food market, rushing to office buildings, or even on supposed weekends at the busy malls - there are people everywhere. And yet, if you sit still for just a minute, in a corner of a mall, or a corner of the food market, and pray the Jesus Prayer, you might just discover where that sacred quiet space is, deep in your heart. It takes some practice to shut out the rush of people around us, the audio and visual stimuli of the noisy conversations around us, but with practice, you will find that inner peace of praying the Jesus Prayer. It is not because we are skilled or talented, but as Saint Macarius the Great said, God's Divine mercy will come to us if we persist in prayer, and grant us that inner joy of prayer eventually.

Our Lord gave the pilgrim yet another spiritual consolation soon after. When he was venerating the relics of Saint Innocent at Irkutsk, a merchant met him and invited him over. The merchant suggested to the pilgrim that he should visit the holy city of Jerusalem, for there are churches and relics of saints aplenty. The pilgrim sadly said that he did not have money to go there. But the merchant told the pilgrim he would write a letter to his son in Odessa, and his son would then arrange for the pilgrim to visit Jerusalem. The pilgrim was overjoyed, and fell at the feet of the kind merchant (Colossians 3:12).

Let us pray unto our Lord, with grateful joy of His many consolations:

> *"Lord Jesus Christ, Son of God,*
> *have mercy on me, a sinner".*

Life and its many Divine signposts

Life is a journey, not just a destination. Do we actively look out for God's subtle signs along our way as His mercies?

Dear beloved,

Our pilgrim recounted to us, his relationship with his spiritual father, whom he communicated with regularly, yet another respected spiritual elder in the pilgrim's life (besides the reposed starets who often appeared to him in dreams).

Often, in our lives, we may lead a sacramental life as faithful Christians, praying at home, reading the Holy Bible and other writings, and attending Church services. However, as we have seen in this book, the pilgrim mentioned many times, the need for a spiritual father in our journey towards God. The spiritual father becomes an available teacher to us, to guide us, to check on our progress, and to help us resist the works of the evil one and his many guises. Often, when people go on their own, it becomes difficult to discern the many subtle Divine signposts intended to guide us, or get easily distracted by the many seemingly pleasant temptations of the devil. While all of us can profess we will resist the devil's works, we are but mere mortals and grave sinners, and our pride and naiveté gets in the way. Therefore, a spiritual father and confessor can be someone we turn to for a prayerful life, as a form of check and balance, as a form of discerning a progressing journey. I have realized that, as the pilgrim did, that it is not easy to find such a spiritual father. But God intends that we take our pilgrimage in life towards Him, seriously (1 Timothy, Titus 1:6-9).

The elder asked about the pilgrim's life, before the pilgrim was to depart from Irkutsk.

The pilgrim then began to reveal his life. He was born in an Orlovsk village. His parents died when he was two years old while his elder brother was ten. His grandparents, an inn owner, cared for them. The pilgrim's elder brother became a wayward drunkard, and caused the pilgrim's left arm to become disabled when the pilgrim was seven years old. Since the pilgrim could not work physical labors anymore, his grandfather taught him to read and write, through the Holy Bible. Eventually, the pilgrim's grandfather was going blind, and it became the pilgrim's turn to read the

Bible to his grandfather. The pilgrim also learned from a county clerk, who had beautiful handwriting. The pilgrim's grandfather told him to be thankful to God, and pray often. Often, the pilgrim would pray, "Have mercy on me, O God". When the pilgrim turned seventeen, his grandmother died. His grandfather insisted that the pilgrim get married, since there was no longer a mistress in the house to tend to family chores. Even though the heart of the pilgrim was against it, his grandfather found him a mature and kind twenty years old lady for him, and they were married.

When the pilgrim was eighteen, sadly, his grandfather died, leaving him the entire inn. His last words were to be a faithful Christian, pray often, attend Church, read the Holy Bible, pray often for his reposed family members, and be kind to the poor.

In life, we are faced with many choices. Sometimes, none of the obvious choices seem to be what we desire or want. However, the consolation I have experienced is that, once we surrender our personal will to God, let go of our egos, vainglory, pretensions, and imagine ourselves, as Adam first was to God, naked, then

God will in His mercy, hold us and lead us back to Him. The pilgrim did not want to be married, but God's will was that he should be at that point in time, to have a consolation in his life, to care for him. If he did not surrender to the Divine will at that point and insisted on not getting married, his life would have gotten worse (Jeremiah 29:11, Proverbs 3 and 15).

However, the wayward elder brother was jealous that their grandfather gave everything to the pilgrim, so his envy raged so much that he burned the inn down and stole everything. The pilgrim and his wife were mercifully spared from the fire, and escaped with their Holy Bible, the very same one his grandfather read to him from. The pilgrim and his wife escaped with only the pajamas on them. They managed to build a small cabin with the help of others, and his wife started to work to support the family, with weaving and sewing. His wife was a pious Christian, and would often be moved to tears as the pilgrim read to her passages in the Holy Bible. Even though they were poor, they kept to their reposed grandfather's advice, to be faithful and prayerful.

What happens when your most trusted people turn against you? Is it not a spiritual struggle of great magnitude? We see in today's highly connected world of social media, quick tempers and transient relationships. "Friendships" seem quick to happen, and yet can disappear like the mist just as quickly. Because of the stressful world we are entrenched in, greed, envy, anger, hatred, and many sins, rise to the surface, brewing like a potent poison, infecting many in the same pot of the world. It is so easy to fall prey to the evil one's temptations and simply allow our fallen selves to take over, and to join in the same path of destruction, hatred, anger, envy, and greed (Romans 1:29, Titus 3:3).

But God intends that we fight against these temptations, to return to the inner cabinet, pray to Him, and surrender our own will of madness. Even if families were to turn against us, the pilgrim and his wife showed us, what pious true Christians should be, without hatred, without anger, only prayer, only charity, only love. High expectations from God no less, but God did not intend us to have a wide and easy path, but a narrow gate (St Matthew 7:13).

The pilgrim was again challenged, when his wife fell ill when he was twenty years old, and died. The pilgrim was then truly alone, and unable to support himself. He took only his most precious possession, his grandfather's Holy Bible, a backpack, and a disability passport (a necessary travel document in those days), and decided to go to Kiev to venerate the relics of saints to ask for intercession. That was thirteen years ago.

The pilgrim's spiritual father exclaimed that the pilgrim, was thirty-three, the age of our Lord Jesus Christ when he was crucified. There are no coincidences in life (Jeremiah 1:4-5).

We are spiritual soldiers, much as Saint Paul the Apostle said. We are to run a marathon of life, to our last breath. We are never to give up on our faith in God, never to give up the pristine heart of Christ we feebly try to imitate, never to fall prey to the many temptations of the evil one (1 Chronicles 28:20, 1 Corinthians 16:13, 2 Timothy 4). We are to fight this inner struggle within our frail bodies and spirits, and to keep vigil, and to pray like Saint Seraphim of Sarov was often depicted, fallen to the ground, with eyes skyward to God, aware of our fallen state, and yet hoping and longing to God, and pray:

> *"Lord Jesus Christ, Son of God,*
> *have mercy on me, a sinner".*

Man proposes, God disposes

Since there are no coincidences in life, even relationships, do we acknowledge God's sovereign will in all things?

Dear beloved,

The pilgrim recounted to his spiritual father, that earlier on, he was hoping to visit the holy city of Jerusalem. He met a friend, who insisted that the pilgrim travel along with an elderly kind gentleman who was quite deaf. The pilgrim at first resisted this offer, because he liked being alone and traveling alone. However, his friend persuaded him that the elderly gentleman would not talk much, and it is unsafe for an old man to travel along a long journey alone. The friend pleaded with the pilgrim for kindness to another fellow being. Finally, the pilgrim agreed.

The pilgrim's spiritual father also commented that in life, there are no coincidences. God has known every one of us before we were born, and He knows exactly what will happen in our lives. He truly is omnipotent and omniscient, for He is the Creator, Lord, and God. Just the other day, my colleagues in the office found that Humans have several blood types, and animals too, have unique blood types, distinct from every other species of animals. Surely such a complex pattern of life is no coincidence or some random event, but speaks of the amazing complexity and sensitivity of God's creation.

The spiritual father was very curious about the pilgrim's journey. However, the pilgrim admitted to his spiritual father that he has forgotten quite many events in his journey, because he would rather focus on the prayer of the heart (Philippians 3:13). The pilgrim recounted that his reposed starets of blessed memory, told him that the evil one would either cause us misery and suffering if we attempt to pray, or if that does not work on us, he would indulge us in pleasant thoughts to distract us from the prayer of the heart. Such spiritual deceptions are the most insidious, and we must always guard against the devil's prelest to prevent sinking into what I consider an endless loop of meaningless "pleasantness", which springs from our own selfish pride, vainglory and greed.

The pilgrim was in need of dried bread when he traveled through the Tobolsk province, and some locals were warm to him, and gave him fresh bread for a whole week, and even gave him a new backpack to replace his broken one.

Later on, the pilgrim met another family, which insisted that the pilgrim rest and eat with them. The master of the house was a judge, and his wife insisted that he stay to chat with her husband. The mistress' mother was a schema nun in Tobolsk and she hoped the pilgrim, while heading back to Irkutsk, would visit the old nun and give her a book of Saint John of the Ladder as a favor. The pilgrim then had dinner with the family and found the family to be pious and good Christians with much respect for everyone, including their helpers. The pilgrim politely asked how the family was so spiritual and kind.

The mistress told the pilgrim that her mother, the schema nun, was the great granddaughter of Saint Joasaph. Their family rented part of their house to a poor nobleman and his family. When the nobleman died, his wife was already pregnant. When the nobleman's wife delivered the baby boy, she died as well. The nobleman's son came into the world an orphan. The mistress' mother adopted the baby boy and raised him as her own. Subsequently the mistress was born a year later.

The two kids grew up and studied together, and eventually, the two of them were married, and the mistress' mother blessed both of them, asked both of them to be faithful and kind Christians to help others, gave the whole estate to both of them, and retired to a monastery as a nun.

The pilgrim sat with the judge in his study and found the study to be a paradise, full of beautiful icons, a life-sized crucifix, Bibles and many books. Both of them sat down to read about prayer together. They focused on the Lord's Prayer (Our Father), which the pilgrim said was the most precious prayer because it came straight from our Lord Jesus Christ.

For many of us, the Lord's Prayer, as with many other liturgical prayers, become but prayers mechanically prayed during liturgies or the daily rule. But do we discern quietly, visit our inner hearts, and feel the Lord's Prayer deep within, and reflect on it with reverence? Have we lost the innocence of a prayerful child so desired by God our Father (St Matthew 18:3)?

In the Philokalia, mentioned by the Pilgrim to the judge and his wife, he recalled that Saint Maximus the Confessor and Saint Peter of

Damascus said that the Lord's Prayer, "Our Father..." asked us to treat others as our own family members, because all of us are truly the children of God. And the verse "Hallowed by Thy Name" reminds us to always take the Name of our Lord in reverence, fear and trembling, and not used it on false oaths. "Thy Kingdom come" reminds us that we can find His kingdom right in our hearts, a tranquil joy found only in the prayer of the heart.

The "daily bread" refers to the Word of God, the very food we need for spiritual fulfillment. Since it is a daily food, it should be consumed regularly (like how many would eat several meals a day), and not taken lightly to read only occasionally. And the Lord's Prayer reminds us to always forgive the sins of others even as we dare to approach God to forgive our many uncountable sins (1 John 1:9). It is important to note that forgiveness is not just an outward verbal expression out of arrogance, but it must come from within as a complete surrender to God's will, to believe God is the only fair judge and the final arbiter of all things, not us (Ephesians 4:32). It also means that to forgive others is to not even have pre-judgment against others, to not view others as any different from us, whatever their race, state of being, situation, wealth, affiliation, and so on (St Luke 6:35). And in the many challenges and trials we face in life, we ask for God's Divine mercy to envelop us, and allow us the mercy to always have the Holy Spirit deep within us, pricking our conscience, opening our hearts to know the many distractions and temptations of the evil one to avoid them.

Let us pray the Lord's Prayer:

"Our Father, Who art in the heavens, hallowed be Thy name. Thy kingdom come, Thy will be done, on earth as it is in heaven. Give us this day our daily bread, and forgive our debts, as we forgive our debtors. And lead us not into temptation, but deliver us from the evil-one. For Thine is the kingdom, and the power, and the glory, forever and ever. Amen".

Let us also remember the prayer of the heart, and let it be like our breathing, our every step, every moment in a day:

"Lord Jesus Christ, Son of God,
have mercy on me, a sinner".

Washing the feet of others in love

Jesus our Lord and Savior, washed the feet of His disciples, paving the way for us to show love to others.

Dear beloved,

The judge and his wife, who were hosting the pilgrim, were kind loving Christians who looked after the weak and the poor. They found the pilgrim lacking socks and had broken shoes, and the judge's wife made a pair of socks and gave a pair of shoes to the pilgrim. The pilgrim at first resisted the kindness, but the kind couple told him that even Jesus Christ washed the feet of His apostles (St John 13:1-17).

Many of us have been exceedingly blessed beyond what we deserve. When we are blessed with a job to feed our families, when we have a roof over our heads, people who care for us, do we appreciate such Divine grace and mercy? What then, do we do with these blessings? Do we hear Christ who said to us, that we would take care of those who are not well, who are poor, who are in need (St Matthew 25:34-40)? We can find many stories of the Holy Unmercenaries, such as Saint Panteleimon from the fourth century, saints who gave their lives to the healing of others without accepting payment. If even Christ our Lord would bend down and wash the feet of His apostles, common men, should we not also follow what He told us to do, to bend ourselves down in true humility, and love those who have been sent our way by God, to be God's saints for us to love?

The kind couple then asked about the life of the pilgrim, and told the pilgrim about a beggar who they once hosted before. The beggar was not well, and as he was dying, asked for a pen and paper, and wrote his last will as a priest heard his confession and administered the mystery of holy unction.

The judge mentioned that the beggar was an educated man, and his will was beautifully written with a good script. The beggar asked the judge to mail the will to his son in Saint Petersburg. After that, the beggar died.

The beggar was a very wealthy prince in his youth. When his wife died, he spent his time with his son, an army captain. One day, due to his foul temper, the prince hit his valet who subsequently died. Soon after, an apparition of the valet kept appearing to the prince day and night, until the prince could no longer function normally. The prince experienced a living hell. The prince finally confessed his sins, and repented, and took on manual labor to atone his terrible sins. When he did that, the apparition of the dead valet disappeared, and the prince found peace in God (St Luke 15:11-32).

This tells us one simple thing, that if we are in a living hell, all of it can be attributed to our own actions, whether it be driven from greed, envy, anger, lust, etc. Conversely, heaven is entirely opposite. What do we keep in our hearts? Do we feel a lightness of being, or a heavy heart? Does what we feel torment us as in hell? Or does what we feel allow us to love God and love others?

Sometimes, in the course of our lives, we may face great depression when we encounter incidents where we are wronged, where we lose loved ones, where we sink into difficulty. We may come into periods of anger, hatred, or frustration. In those times, we will experience moments or even long periods of dark nights. However, those are nights to cleanse us, where we can be reconciled back to God, where He has been there all along, waiting for us. If we do not cross the desert, how would we find the oasis? Often, if we were to find true inner peace through prayer unto God, in hindsight, we would have noticed that those were times meant for spiritual formation, through reflection, study, and prayer. Those would be great moments in our lives intended for us to release our emotional and spiritual burdens unto God, to repent for our emotional weaknesses such as anger and hatred, and find comfort in Him (2 Peter 3:9).

The last will of the prince to his son was to confess his youthful mistakes, and that he died in the home of a kindly benefactor (the judge). He wrote to his son to be mindful of God, be mindful of his actions, to be kind to everyone, and to pray for him (2 Maccabees 12:44-45).

The pilgrim was very gratified at the kindness of the judge and his family towards anyone, especially the poor. But he wondered if there had been troublemakers in the past.

The judge was very wise. To him, he did not care if anyone were to take advantage of his kindness - his kindness was extended equally to all who accepted it.

It is easy to desire to care for the little children of the world, who are helpless and innocent. However, the judge and his family showed us what true Christian love was - universal. They would care for anyone who came to them, regardless of whether they were drunkards or sober, courteous or disorderly. Likewise, as we look around us, often some who need our help the most, may not be in a pleasant situation, and in turn, would show anger, frustration, hatred, or even malice. But Christ called us to care for the least among us, and those who are trapped in a living hell, are also the least among us. Our "feet washing" for others, should be universal towards all who are in need, even if they may not acknowledge this need out of pride. Let us always attempt to humble ourselves, to see all in the image of Christ, no matter how they appear to us.

Let us always be mindful of the prayer of the heart, that reminds us of our fallen state, and that only our Lord Jesus Christ will be our light back to God:

> *"Lord Jesus Christ, Son of God,*
> *have mercy on me, a sinner".*

True humility & spiritual journeys

Lest we misjudge good people, let us remember the saints sometimes present guises out of true humility.

Dear beloved,

The pilgrim joined the judge's family to the Divine Liturgy at the community church. The pilgrim was so moved that the family and the kids would kneel and pray, with tears of joy on their faces, whose radiance made the pilgrim cry with tears of joy too. The family showed their faith through actions, not just a mental agreement with the Truth (St James 2:14-19, Romans 10:10).

Every Divine Liturgy is our blessing to be able to partake in the Divine Nature. It is a unique Holy Mystery that allows us, the living, to partake in unified worship with the hosts and the departed, towards God. It is the central activity in the Church that unites all of us faithful. When we attend the Divine Liturgy, it gives us a foretaste of heaven, and makes us feel infinitely small and transparent before God, and yet, powerfully warm, like a cuddled baby, in the cradle of God (2

Thessalonians 2:14).

When we attend the Liturgy of Preparation, we are made aware of the entry prayers, we venerate the icons of our Lord and Christ and our Holy Theotokos. Our priests are vested with the solemnity of understanding God's grace and mercy of using humble laborers to serve His Divine purpose and celebration.

And when we partake in the Liturgy of the Word, we remember the importance of the Holy Word of God, and we remember Christ Himself. We pray the litanies, Psalms, Beatitudes, Trisagion, Epistles, Gospels, and listen to the Homily of the day. It is a celebration of our faith in God, a celebration of the Word made known to us through Christ and His apostles, and a celebration of the Divine inspiration through the Holy Spirit.

When we attend, with fear and trembling, and with much longing, the Liturgy of the Faithful, we profess our faith universally through the Creed, Sursum Corda, commemoration of the saints, the Lord's Prayer, and we partake in receiving the Holy Communion of the Body and Blood of Christ, a Holy Mystery that we are blessed to receive (St Matthew 26:26-28).

After the Liturgy, the pilgrim was shocked that the priest said that he did not have time for reading the saints' writings, due to his many duties. However, the judge's wife told the pilgrim that he should not misinterpret the priest's true humility as one of nonchalance. The pilgrim humbly reflected on the sayings of Nikitas Stethatos in the Philokalia, that a person is measured from the interior soul, and not what is manifested on the outside, or said. The pilgrim further reflected that the truly prayerful and faithful Christian, especially one who has genuine inner prayer and love for others, would love all equally, saints and sinners alike. Just as many things grow in silence, the greatest of saints around us, may well be those who are meek, silent, and seemingly obscure (St James 3:2). Just as we need a silent heart to listen to the heartbeat of God, stop and listen quietly, and pray quietly, and we might just discover the subtle and gentle signs of God around us, and in the people around us (St Matthew 14:23).

Saint Dorotheus of Gaza once said, "Through the mercy of God, the little things done with humility will enable us to be found in the same place as the saints who have labored much and were true servants of God."

The pilgrim also saw a blind beggar at Church, who prayed the Jesus Prayer unceasingly for a long time, despite his disability. The pilgrim also took to inner prayer, basking in the true joy and tranquility, inspired by the blind beggar's faith. The blind beggar told the pilgrim he was once a tailor, who loved to pray the Jesus Prayer. However, his vocal prayers perturbed people around him, and so eventually the tailor prayed without moving his lips, letting the Jesus Prayer encircle silently in his heart instead. One day, the tailor became blind, but continued to pray from the heart, the Jesus Prayer.

When we are struck with calamities, or suffering challenges in life, do we relieve ourselves of the emotional and physical burdens and leave them with God, and brave on as Saint Paul admonished us to as soldiers or marathon runners? Do we lose our faith in difficulties and blame God, or do we see Divine reason and pray and trust Him all the more (1 Corinthians 10:13, Revelation 3:21)?

The pilgrim was grateful of the company of the

blind beggar, and so both of them set off together, and the pilgrim read the Philokalia to the blind man along their journey, as they prayed together.

If we are truly blessed with faith, with the Word of God, with the many illuminations, do we keep them to ourselves? Or do we willingly share such inner joy with others who come to us? Even as we are unworthy sinners, perhaps we can pray unto God and ask our Lord for His mercy and grace to embrace us, to grant us the ability to share His truth and love with others. Our tongues are frail, our minds are feeble, and our spirits weak. But surely God has infinite wisdom, strength and love that can shine through us, His children (Hebrews 10:25)?

Let us pray:

> *"Lord Jesus Christ, Son of God,*
> *have mercy on me, a sinner".*

Identifying true fruits of prayer

What are the signs of true inner prayer? What are its fruits? How do we deal with visions during prayer?

Dear beloved,

Our pilgrim has been traveling with a blind man for a while, and both of them prayed together, while the pilgrim read the Philokalia to the blind man. The pilgrim then taught a way to approach the Jesus Prayer to the blind man.

The pilgrim asked the blind man to visualize the heart within his chest cavity, and listen with his ears every heart beat. Then repeat the Jesus Prayer in tandem with the heartbeat. With the first heartbeat, mentally (or verbally) say "Lord". The second beat, say "Jesus", the third beat, "Christ", and so on. Then regulate the breathing in tandem with the Prayer, with "Lord Jesus Christ" through an inhalation, and "have mercy on me" with exhalation. The pilgrim then mentioned that soon, if one persisted with such prayer, one should feel a tender soreness and warmth in the heart.

However, the pilgrim warned the blind man that unlike other methods, the Orthodox prayer must be void of imagination or visions. One must reject all manners of created imagination, according to the teachings of the Holy Fathers, who said that imagination can lead to prelest (spiritual deception).

Shortly after, the blind man suddenly said to the pilgrim that he saw a vision of a nearby church burning. The pilgrim told the blind man to leave aside all imaginations, which are temptations. When both of them walked to the village, they saw the church burned down. The pilgrim told the blind man that even as the vision came true, one must NOT see visions as a direct correlation to Divine grace, but as natural occurrences that may be led by carnal passions. The blind man was humbled by the pilgrim's teachings, and went back to prayer with gratefulness.

Saint John Cassian the Roman said, "We will most easily come to a precise knowledge of true discernment if we follow the paths of our elders, if we do nothing novel, and if we do not presume to decide anything on the basis of our own private judgment."

The two people parted company at Tobolsk while the pilgrim continued on his journey.

The pilgrim continued to pray unceasingly, and soon, he experienced blessed joy and tranquility, as if in the Kingdom of Heaven. His perspective of surroundings and people began to change. He started to see all things, people, flora, and fauna, with a positive light, that all of these things were sealed in the Name of Jesus Christ. He began to feel as though his body carried no physical weight.

Saint John of Konstadt said, "Love every person despite his falling into sin. Look past the person's sins, and remember that the foundation of the person is the same - the image of God".

The fruits of our prayerful labors can be discerned thus. Do we love all of God's creation - regardless of race, religion, or condition (Genesis 1:31, Job 41:11)? Do we love God's other creations - plants, animals, earth, etc (Leviticus 26:3-4)? Do we become blind to judging others?

But yet, just as he admonished the blind man on visions, the pilgrim too, began to realize that spiritual consolations are not to be indulged.

When he felt anxiety and fear later on, he would pray more seriously, and thoughts of fear subsided.

For us, we must also remember that God's will is to temper us, as a jeweler, to forge strength and beauty out of us (Ephesians 2:10). God's will is not to satiate us or to placate us that will turn us into sloppy creatures. Only the devil will attempt to satiate our lusts and passions, and to pacify us with easy journeys.

Let us pray unto God, to lead us into true inner prayer, and grant us Divine Mercy not to fall into prelest:

> *"Lord Jesus Christ, Son of God,*
> *have mercy on me, a sinner".*

Responsibilities, fears, & time

How do we view our responsibilities? How do we alleviate our fears? How do we view worship and liturgies?

Dear beloved,

The pilgrim walked through a heavy rain for two days, and became exhausted. Eventually, he found a small farmhouse manned by a drunken old man, and asked if he could stay the night. The old man was a postmaster and the farmhouse was the community post office. The postmaster checked through the pilgrim's passport and permitted him to stay. The postmaster's cook was a young lady, and made a bed for the pilgrim.

Deep in the night, some loud crashing noises woke the postmaster's cook up in frightful terror. The pilgrim and the postmaster both also woke up, and all three of them discovered that a royal courier crashed from his horse carriage, with a stake through his head. Even with the serious injury, the royal courier braved on, and galloped off, intending to carry out his job responsibilities (2 Timothy 2:15).

Six years later, the pilgrim prayed at a women's monastery. A humble nun poured tea for the pilgrim. Then the pilgrim realized the nun was the young cook who worked for the postmaster six years ago. After her frightful encounter with the royal courier's injury, she was so frightened she went insane. Her family brought her from monastery to monastery to no avail, until she was brought to the monastery where she was healed (Proverbs 29:25). She gave her life to God, and became a nun.

The pilgrim journeyed on, and on one summer day, he heard the bells of a church, and went in to attend the Divine Liturgy. A young, frail priest celebrated the Liturgy very slowly. The pilgrim was very moved by the slow, faithful way the young priest served the Liturgy. The priest told the pilgrim, that even though his parishioners disliked his ways, he loved to reflect on every word of the Divine Liturgy, and savor the whole experience with inner reflection and prayer. The pilgrim wondered how could one find this inner enlightenment. The priest explained that one needs to take a single passage from the Holy Bible, meditate and spend time on that single passage, and take as long as needed, and God will shine His light to allow one to understand it. The same thing goes for prayer as well. Prayer cannot be rushed, or cavalier, but must be savored and reflected slowly, as long as it takes.

I would humbly make an analogy that the study of Holy Scriptures and prayer should be like expensive caviar, something you would enjoy and experience slowly, not rushed through. It should not be rushed through like a chore or fast food. Prayer, like the study of Holy Scriptures, is a labor of love. It needs tremendous effort, especially to fend off the many distractions, delusions, and temptations of the evil one. It will be an uphill climb, but thoroughly worth every effort (St Mark 11:22-25).

After dinner, the pilgrim overheard an old lady whispering the Jesus Prayer. He was very moved by the piety of the old lady. The old lady replied that the only joy she could experience at her age was to seek God's forgiveness. She had been praying the Jesus Prayer since she was a little girl, and she could not do without the Jesus Prayer. When she was a young lady, her parents wanted to give her away in marriage, but the groom-to-be died suddenly and she decided to lead a celibate life and prayed unceasingly.

Not all of us have the blessing to pray unceasingly yet. But it would be a sensible question to ask ourselves - do we ask God's forgiveness only at the end of our journey in life? Or should we start now, and do it often while acknowledging Him as our Lord and Savior (Ezekiel 18:30)? We will never know the hour of our death, so let us always pray to Him, every breath, every heartbeat, every step. Let not our youth or old age, fit or unfit, stop us.

A soldier once asked Abba Mius if God would accept the repentance of sinners. Abba Mius asked the soldier if his cloak is torn, would he throw it away? The soldier replied, "No. I will mend it and wear it again." Abba Mius then said, "If you would mend your cloak and wear it again, wouldn't God care a lot more about His precious creation?"

The pilgrim journeyed on, and met a retired captain and chatted with him on prayer. The captain relied on the writings of Saint Gregory Palamas, father among the saints. The pilgrim suggested the captain read the Philokalia, which went further from the oral form of the Jesus

Prayer in Saint Gregory Palamas' writings, to the complete and perfected teaching on the inner spiritual Jesus Prayer. Such is the fullness of the faith in the Orthodox Church, and the many splendors of a wide spectrum of available teachings from various fathers of the Church, all Divinely inspired by the Holy Spirit through 2,000 unbroken years of Church history.

The pilgrim thanked his spiritual father after relating all his journeying stories, and said he would continue to make his way to Jerusalem. His spiritual father blessed him, and wished that God's grace would be with the pilgrim, just as Saint Raphael the Archangel journeyed with Tobit and his son Tobias (Tobit 12:14-15). Saint Raphael the Archangel is the protector of pilgrims and their prayers, and brings God's healing to God's children.

As we close with our reflection of "The Way of a Pilgrim", let us pray:

> *"Lord Jesus Christ, Son of God,*
> *have mercy on me, a sinner".*

The mysteries of Divine Will

When we are confronted with personal choices, do we sometimes try to force our own will on impossible situations? Why not surrender to Divine Will instead?

Dear beloved,

Let us now read from the second book, "The Pilgrim continues his way."

A year has passed since we last heard of the pilgrim. He is reunited with his spiritual father. The pilgrim reported to the elder, that despite his own wish to visit Jerusalem, it was not to be.

The pilgrim was to travel with the deaf old man to Odessa via Irkutsk, through an introduction letter from a merchant to his son. However, to the pilgrim's dismay, when he reached Odessa, the merchant's son has died of a sudden illness. The household of the merchant's family was exceedingly kind to allow the pilgrim to stay for two months, despite them being in mourning. Then, the merchant in Irkutsk wrote to his son's family in Odessa, to all go back to Irkutsk without delay. Something important or terrible must have happened to the kind merchant in Irkutsk, and so, the pilgrim, had no reason to impose on the good people in Odessa, and moved on to continue his travels in Russia.

Such is the Divine Will in many of life's events. When we insist on something in our own strength and will, we often face tremendous obstacles. These obstacles might be God's Divine signals to us not to proceed foolishly with some bad decisions in our lives. I have humbly found, through my own challenges in life, that as soon as I surrender to the Will of God, in situations of danger, difficulty, or temptation, the path becomes easier to understand, and sometimes, easier to bear as well. After all, God has known us before we are born. He would know our lives throughout our journeys, even before we make many foolish decisions. After all, when we profess the Lord's Prayer, do we not take this instrumental and universal Christian prayer seriously (St Matthew 6:10)?

The pilgrim saw a peasant of good standing, wanting to commit suicide, because he felt great pain and suffering and wanted to end it all. He was rescued and was recuperating in hospital. The pilgrim told the peasant and his family, that one should always go to God in prayer first, and to confide their woes to family members and trustworthy friends, so that one would not give in to the evil one's snares of suicide (1 Corinthians 12:12-26).

In life, we often need to do two things as Christ commanded: (1) Love God, and (2) love others as ourselves. Likewise, in many activities in life for us who are deep in the world, we need two things also, (a) Prayer, and (b) People.

The pilgrim mentioned that God treasures every seemingly small deed done for Him, whether it is an action, or even an intention, that serves to glorify Him. The Holy Spirit warms us to such good intentions or good actions for God, and grieves when we turn away.

"No good deed, no matter how insignificant it may be, will be scorned by the Righteous Judge" - Saint John Chrysostom, father among the saints.

For those of us who are blessed with much, God demands much from us. For those of us who are blessed with less, do not lament, for God does not simply weigh you on the weight of gold and silver, but your heart (2 Corinthians 5:17).

The pilgrim told us another story, of a monk

who lived a good life, and gave in to the temptation of wanting to eat dried fish. The monk went to the city to buy dried fish, but discovered he forgot to bring his chotki. Just as he was about to turn back, he found his chotki in his pocket. He made the Sign of the Cross and continued to walk to the marketplace. When the monk reached there, a horse near a crate load of goods went berserk and knocked him down, and tripped the heavy crate over. Blessedly, the crate crashed besides the monk and did not kill him. The monk still purchased the dried fish and went back to his monastery. Later in the night, the monk dreamed of the patron of the monastery, who chided him on his weakness against his lusts and his laziness in striving for understanding and strength. The patron of the monastery told the monk in his dream, that it was due to the guardian angel who inspired the monk to remember his chotki as a mark of a monk, and to remember to pray and make the Sign of the Cross, which lent God's mercy to prevent certain death. When the monk woke up, he was not on the bed, but prostrated near the door, just as he dreamed.

God gives us many signs in our journey, and the more aggressive the attacks of the evil one against our rather weak souls, the more pressing His Divine intervention. However, many of us rely on our own will and strength, and neglect to notice the many signs He has given us (St James 4:1-10). Let us always remember to look around for His saving hints, to look beyond the flaws of people around us who bear the image of Christ and His love by giving us loving guidance, and most of all, let us pray to God to grant us mercy so that we can see His signs at all times, throughout our lives, so that we may be able to stand before His throne and worship Him day and night in His temple (Revelation 7:13-17).

"Prayer cleanses instantly, though it may be uttered by us who are filled with sin." - Saint John Chrysostom, father among the saints.

Let us pray for an open and gentle heart that will be sensitive to God's Will:

> *"Lord Jesus Christ, Son of God,*
> *have mercy on me, a sinner".*

Humble, down-to-earth confessions

While we remember the importance of the mystery of reconciliation, how should we confess?

Dear beloved,

Saint John Cassian the Roman defined the eight evil vices, in the Philokalia, namely: Gluttony, luxury, avarice, wrath, sloth, negligence, vainglory and pride. The most important thing for us is to recognize these sins when they arise, whether in actions, or in our intent, and then to stop these sins and reconcile back to God by going to confession, the holy mystery of reconciliation.

The pilgrim wanted to partake the holy mystery of the Communion, and so, he needed to go to confession (St John 20:22-23). The pilgrim wrote down every single sin in great detail, and ended up with a long list. He traveled a few miles away to the Kitayev Hermitage in Kiev.

The elder at the Kitayev Hermitage looked at the long detailed list of the pilgrim, and gave some solemn advice on what a confession should

NOT be.

1. One should not confess against sins that have previously been confessed and absolved by a priest, or it should imply a lack of faith on the mystery of reconciliation.

2. One should only confess sins relating to oneself, and never accuse others in one's confession.

3. One should not detail sins too much, but only in very general terms, as forbidden by the Holy Fathers, because too much details may lead one and his confessor into temptation, since many sins are carnal and lustful in nature.

4. One should not repent with detachment, as if one is merely an observer to the sins, but must repent as one means it.

5. One should always remember the most important sins, that of not loving God, not loving our neighbors, not believe the Holy Scripture, and that one is filled with pride and greed. These are the fundamental sins that drive all other manners of sins and woes.

After that, the elder explained what true confession should be, and how such a confession would nurture humility in a person, by sharing his own confession with the pilgrim.

A. I do not love God. Because if I truly love God, I would think of God the whole day and not get tired, and would pray, obey and glorify Him the whole day with joy (St John 14:23).

B. I do not love my neighbors as myself. Because if I did, I would carry the burden of others' worries, and take care of them as I would for my own burdens, and I would share in the joy of others as much as I rejoice in my own.

C. I have no faith in Holy Scripture. Because if I did, I would believe in the salvation Christ pointed us to through His Word, and in the caring for this life to prepare for our afterlife.

D. I am full of pride and greed. That is why I would boast of needless things to others, display however little I have to snub others, to defend my sins with excuses, and even do charity for the sake of praise or social standing. I am worshipping myself rather than God.

The pilgrim was so moved to shame, but so thankful to the elder at the hermitage.

Saint Maximus the Confessor said in the

Philokalia, "Every genuine confession humbles the soul. When it takes the form of thanksgiving, it teaches the soul that it has been delivered by the grace of God."

Much as the Jesus Prayer is a profession of our faith in Christ our Lord, it is also a confessional prayer. Let us pray:

"Lord Jesus Christ, Son of God,
have mercy on me, a sinner".

God loves penitent prayers

God loves prayer, and especially when we go to Him to repent of our many sins. Are we able to let our pride go and confess?

Dear beloved,

Our pilgrim met a Greek monk from Mount Athos, who fell ill during his trip to Russia to raise funds for his monastery. The pilgrim decided to look after the Greek monk, pro bono. The pilgrim found great spiritual joy as both of them read from the Philokalia, and prayed often (Proverbs 13:20).

The Greek monk said of the Jesus Prayer, that it is of 2 parts, (1) "Lord Jesus Christ, Son of God" contains the entire Gospel according to the Holy Fathers and the history of Christ, as it affirms the Lordship of Jesus, who is our Messiah, and the Son of God, part of the Trinity - representing the salvation from God; and (2) "have mercy on me, a sinner" contains an abbreviated overtone of our own history, one full of sins and foolishness. So when we place Christ's history sovereign above our sinful own, we are acknowledging Him as our salvation of all our sins. The Greek monk also mentioned that while we are asking Christ for mercy, we are not approaching out of fear, but out of love and tears of joy, as a child to his Father (1 Peter 5:7).

One day, a Christian visited the Greek monk and the pilgrim, and complained about Jews who ill-treated and cheated him. The Greek monk told the Christian, that one should respect and love ALL of God's creatures, and should pray for those who may have wronged us (Psalm 140:1-4 LXX). The Greek monk read to the Christian, from the writings of Saint Mark the Ascetic:

"One who has interior union with God, having experienced tremendous joy, will be kind, unassuming, and non-judgmental against anyone, whether Greek, pagan, Jew, sinners alike. This person will view everyone equally and with purity, with much joy for the world, and pray that everyone, Greeks, Jews, and pagans will glorify God."

"Contemplatives burn with so much love that, if at all possible, they would embrace everyone into their bosoms, whether good or evil" - Saint Macarius the Great (Coptic).

We pale in comparison, and are deeply ashamed should we dare to stand before these saints today, in a conversation. Much as we try to love our neighbors as ourselves while professing our love for God, or even attempt to try to forgive and love our "enemies", we know inside our hearts that we are far from the advice given out of love to us, from holy elders such as Saint Macarius and Saint Mark the Ascetic (St Matthew 22:39).

When the Greek monk recovered, the pilgrim took his leave and journeyed on. Soon a deserter met the pilgrim and asked for his counsel. The deserted recounted his story, that he took the identity of an honorably discharged dead soldier, and married the widowed daughter of an old trader. When the old trader died, the deserter and his wife ruined the business to the ground, due to their ignorance of doing business. Eventually, out of poverty and hunger, the deserter started stealing. One day, he dreamt of his dead grandfather, who in the dream, wanted to kill him for his sins. When he woke up from his dreams, there were physical signs of struggle that matched what he dreamed about, and he was deeply distressed and afraid. Finally, unable to deal with his guilt, he wanted to hang himself, and that's when he met the pilgrim (Psalm 49:15 LXX, Isaiah 61:1-3).

The pilgrim told the deserter, that he should pray to God to quash the fears and anger. But the deserter was afraid to pray, that God would strike him down for the terrible sins he had committed. The pilgrim assured the deserter that God would forgive one who will repent and pray for his sins. The pilgrim suggested the deserter start praying the Jesus Prayer. The two of them walked and prayed together towards Pochaev. The pilgrim told the deserter that both of them should receive the communion. The deserted listened, and went to confession, receive the Holy Communion, and prayed the Jesus Prayer unceasingly. One day, he fell asleep and dreamt that his grandfather appeared in glory, with much love, told him to get a job at the Church of Saint George the Conqueror in Zhitomir, and live out his life. Such is the mercy of God when we repent of our sins (Ephesians 3:12).

Many of the greatest saints did not start out as saints. And God does not give up on any of His creations. If we are willing to step up to Him, with true humility, leave our burdens with Him, and confess all of our sins in tears, God will listen to a penitent confession and prayer. Let us pray:

"Lord Jesus Christ, Son of God,
have mercy on me, a sinner".

The Gospels on inner prayer

When we think of prayer, is it only about
satisfying our desires? How then, should
we really pray to God?

Dear beloved,

The pilgrim attended a Divine Liturgy in church, and got acquainted with a nobleman. Both of them decided to travel together to visit the Slovetsky Monastery and pray there.

The pilgrim noticed that the nobleman was always reading the Holy Bible and asked him which scriptural texts inspired him the most. The nobleman then explained that he read the entire New Testament from beginning to end. The pilgrim asked the nobleman how best to read the Holy Bible to pray better.

The nobleman told the pilgrim to read Gospel of Saint Matthew, on how to prepare for prayer, intended for beginners, such that one should never pray from vanity; and to pray in a quiet place away from noise (Philippians 4:6-7). One should pray only for the Lord's forgiveness of one's sins and to walk closer to God, and not to petition for things or needs like pagans (St Matthew 6:5-8).

Then one should understand what prayerful words are, such that one must first forgive others truly, before we dare to approach God for His forgiveness of our own sins. We should also understand that pray is about consistency and steadfast effort with much hope, and not expect God to be a tap that we turn on anytime we want for our needs, or expect God to be an instant fast food delivery. God has His own will and reasons, a mystery we will never understand (St Matthew 6:9-13, 7:7-12, St Mark 14:32-40, St Luke 11:5-14 and 18:3-7).

The nobleman explained that the Gospel of Saint John contained much of the mysteries of the prayer of the heart. We are reminded of the conversation between Jesus Christ and the Samaritan lady, where we learned that the inner worship of God must be centered in truth, and complete in the Holy Spirit (Ephesians 6:18, Hebrews 1:20-21, and Romans 8:26), because that is what God desires of us. In the same Gospel, we learned that true unceasing prayer must be like an ever-flowing stream of water, much like everlasting life (1 Thessalonians 5:17).

The Gospel of Saint John also described that state of inner prayer as one that has an eternal remembrance of God (St John 4:5-16, 15:4-8).

We are told that whatever we ask of God in the name of our beloved Lord and Christ, God will give us (St John 16:23-25). But does Christ mean for us to ask God for favors, gifts, and things we selfishly lust after?

All too often, many failed to understand the nature of prayer, and instead, made endless petitions to God, hoping to be satiated of their desires and lusts. God certainly has limitless power to fulfill anything, but He fulfills prayers that will draw us closer to Him. Many people seem to remember God, and render a cavalier "thanks" to God, when they experienced some good blessings. But do we remember God in every breath, every step, every action, and every consequence in our lives? In the good, and the very bad, do we think of God, and thank Him for Divine providence that leads us to Him, and not merely expecting to be spoon fed with miracles, wonders, gifts, and showers of gold?

Do we remember to pray for the needs of others (1 Timothy 2:1-5), as we often ask our Most

Holy Theotokos, the archangels, the blessed saints, to pray for us as well?

Let us pray, thinking of the specific needs of people around us, for Divine will and mercy to embrace us, with the aching heart of a loving brother or sister:

"Lord Jesus Christ, Son of God, have mercy on us, sinners all".

Meeting of spiritual minds

As Christ promised, a gathering of Christ-minded people will grow spiritually together, and pray powerfully together.

Dear beloved,

The pilgrim met his spiritual father together with a professor, a priest, and a skhimnik (a Russian Orthodox monk of strict observance, akin to say, Roman Catholic Trappist monks).

The professor first started with his story. He was leading a luxurious and wasteful life. He met a young Frenchman who wanted to introduce him to some amoral activities one day, at the professor's study. The young man told the professor that both of them should continue discussing their activities outside the study instead. The professor was puzzled and asked why. The young man said that there was a New Testament sitting in the professor's study, and he felt uncomfortable discussing amoral activities in front of the Holy Scripture. The professor took the New Testament, and handed to the young man to put it in another room. As soon as the young man came into contact with the Holy Book, he trembled, and disappeared!

The professor was shocked and fainted, and when he woke up, his limbs were paralyzed and had to lie in bed. He resigned from his teaching position after his mother died and his sister entered a monastery. Despite all these traumatic experiences, the New Testament was frequently in the professor's hands. One day, a hermit came, and told the professor to trust in the mercy of God through prayer, rather than rely on medicines. The professor prayed, and his symptoms of trauma and depression subsided.

The skhimnik commented that the professor was an educated man and so should not fall into despair, especially after the immense mercy and healing from God (Hebrews 11:6).

"No one should despair and proclaim the Gospel to be unattainable. In laying the foundation for man's salvation, God did not issue commandments intending them to be impossible to attain so that man would turn to sin, but rather, are intended that through a journey to holiness through the commandments, we will be blessed while living and in eternity." - Saint John

Chrysostom, father among the saints, often called the "Golden Mouth".

The skhimnik lamented that contemporary preaching of the Gospel seemed to gravitate between promises of bliss and rewards, and that of hell and brimstone. I humbly also submit, that the skhimnik's lament still holds true today.

The skhimnik then referred to the Philokalia as the reference for the nature of prayer and how best to pray. While some may imagine prayer to be complex and esoteric, the Holy Fathers in the Philokalia gave a layered teaching, that prayer can be simple, or deep. According to the Fathers, true prayer should restrain and focus the mind and our memory to constantly remember God, of journeying with Him and feeling His presence, of loving Him, and calling His Holy Name through the Name of Jesus Christ our beloved Lord and Savior, during any and all moments of our lives.

Some of us might then imagine that we should summon our strength and will to "grow faith" in God. However, the Holy Bible detailed that even if we are to try, we cannot even have faith the size of a mustard seed. This is because faith, unlike our own will, is a tremendous gift from God, granted through the Holy Spirit. So the more we pray, no matter how simple, the more we grow in the comfort of the Holy Spirit, and the stronger our faith may be.

"To pray constantly in any manner is within our will, but true prayer is a gift of grace" - Saint Hesychius.

"When the soul is clouded by unclean thoughts, flog the enemies with the Name of Jesus constantly, as it is the strongest weapon in heaven and on earth" - Saint John Climacus, of the Ladder.

On top of faith, we are also told to nurture acts of faith for the good of others (St Matthew 19:17-19, St James 2:10). We are to show genuine love and concern for others, especially not forgetting those in need. We cannot be selfish and profess to have faith in God, because God is selfless, and full of love. Again, like faith, acts of kindness cannot be a pretentious and egoistic activity that we derive out of our own will, but we must pray hard so that God will gift us with faith and the heart of compassion for acting towards fulfilling the needs of others. Often, the best evangelism is through good works of compassion towards others and living in the ways of Christ, and not "hell-and-brimstone" evangelism.

Let us pray to God, through the mercy of Jesus Christ our Lord, for faith of an unmovable rock, and the gentle heart full of compassion and love for others in need:

"Lord Jesus Christ, Son of God,
have mercy on me, a sinner".

God's love transcends our condition

Whatever our condition, wise or simple,
brash or meek, God loves us all, especially
if we make that step towards Him,
through prayer.

Dear beloved,

The skhimnik went on to describe the important things when praying constantly. First, any thought or subtle stirring of true prayer is a result of the work of the Holy Spirit and one's guardian angel (Exodus 23). Second, the Name of Jesus Christ in the prayer effects beneficial powers in it. Third, trust in calling the Name of Jesus Christ in the prayer, and ignore one's own failure in praying, or the criticism of other people in your attempts to pray unceasingly.

Sometimes, the evil one may provoke our envy for others with spiritual gifts. But beloved, do consider that God loves us all despite our failings, and He has Divine plans for every one of His creation, whatever our gifts He mercifully gave us. Saint John of Karpathos in the Philokalia mentioned that even if we do not have discipline in fasting or attain spiritual feats, our Lord will still want to save us through our prayer.

Very few of us are to be monks living a cloistered life, which in a pristine environment, is a special gift to be able to pray unceasingly in silence. Many of us are deep in the world, living among people and environments, challenged often by our surroundings.

Still, the skhimnik reminded us that whether we are monks or not, we are to try to pray unceasingly, because our feeble attempts to pray will be warmly welcomed by God, and He in turn, will grant us unceasing prayer when we try enough. For example, the skhimnik mentioned Patriarch Photius who, despite being a busy hierarch overseeing the diocese of Constantinople, he was able to pray unceasingly. Saint Callistus of Mount Athos was also able to pray unceasingly despite handling the kitchen chores as a cook. Many people, despite having a busy and hurried life, could find in their hearts, the desire to pray unceasingly. Should we not attempt leaning on the heartbeat of our beloved God in our daily journey of life too?

The priest then said to the skhimnik that Holy

Scripture mentioned that verbal prayer alone was useless without proper attention of the heart (St Matthew 15:8, 7:21). The skhimnik clarified that the Holy Scripture should be interpreted to mean the hypocritical worship unto God without a true intention and flaunting such worship to others, as the Pharisees Christ mentioned. The skhimnik agreed that if one does not treat prayer like a disciplined exercise that is exercised consistently, frequently, with strength, over a sustained period of time, then prayer will not encircle within one's heart to be unceasing. The more one prays, the more the Holy Spirit will provide the strength to carry on in prayer, until it becomes unceasing.

The skhimnik mentioned that prayer in itself, especially that of calling the Name of Jesus Christ, would have the mystery of a power that drives one to be on the road to righteousness by banishing evil thoughts, disasters, calamities, even our passions, by the mercy of God (1 John 4:4). And prayer should be energized by an inner love within oneself. With love, God is pleased, and He will make all things happen for one's journey closer to Him. Without love, all efforts are futile.

But as a warning, we are also reminded by the professor to pray unto God out of love, and NOT out of spiritual gluttony or attachment for fruits and rewards (St Matthew 19:21).

Dear beloved, with a humble heart, with no expectation of fruits, but just a love for our Lord, let us pray:

*"Lord Jesus Christ, Son of God,
have mercy on me, a sinner".*

Praying in solitude and silence

*Do we spend "we" time with God every
day, or even every breath? Do we, like
Christ, take time off from tasks to pray in
solitude to God?*

Dear beloved,

The pilgrim and the professor was about to bid
farewell to the spiritual father at the monastery,
when the pilgrim's spiritual father said that a
Moldavian monk and a hermit would like to meet
and chat with both of them. So they stayed.

The pilgrim said that if he had sufficient
money, he would have become a hermit too, as
being a solitary is a tremendous blessing to
Theosis without distractions. However, the
professor's view counter-balanced the pilgrim's,
that everything in life may appear to be good from
a distance. There are always advantages, and
disadvantages, especially if we take the time to
dwell deep in it. The professor reminded the
pilgrim that there were many hermits and ascetics
who fell into egoistic delusions as well. The
pilgrim concurred that to be true, as he had seen

even those who experienced unceasing prayer of the heart fell into despair and abandoned their faith. Therefore, the lesson in life can be simple. Do we love God above ourselves, and that we recognize we are nothing without the salvation of Christ the Word, the comfort and guiding of the Holy Spirit, and the Divine Mercy of our Father above?

The hermit clarified and added to what both the pilgrim and the professor said, that if one chooses to be a hermit, it was absolutely important that one has a spiritual director to help one nurture and grow the faith and the inner prayer unto God, to prevent the ego and delusions from attacking oneself (Proverbs 13:20, 1 Thessalonians 5:14). This advice holds true for the faithful like us, who are deep in the world, in touch with communities, and yet sought the inner prayerful life towards Theosis with God, as we too, are solitaries when we pray in the closet (St Matthew 6:6).

"A true and knowledgeable spiritual director is necessary for the interior life. Sought one if one does not yet have one. But if one cannot be found, pray with tears to God, that the writings of the Holy Fathers can guide oneself, and to rely on the

Holy Bible as the compass" - Saint Nicephorus the Hermit.

The hermit gave a profound teaching that is most illuminating in our search for God among His creation. He said that, when one seeks God with a true heart, one can find good useful advice from anyone. The hermit quoted that the Holy Fathers said that even if one turns to a Saracen (i.e. a non-believer) with faith in God and the right intention, even such a person can render valuable advice. Likewise, the Fathers said that if one turns to a Prophet without faith and right intentions, one will deride the Prophet and think his advice is useless. Therefore, let us consider, beloved, that God's grace and mercy is above all that we can imagine. He is not confined or restrained by our microscopic minds, nor defined by us His full extent and possibilities of His salvation to be given to all His creation. He alone will and can decide how, when, and where He save any one of us (1 John 3:20, St Matthew 19:26). He will, as can be shown throughout human history, use ANYONE as His instrument for good and deliverance of His people. This is exactly why Christ commanded us above all things, to (1) love God, and (2) love others as ourselves.

The professor wondered if repentance would be the cure to preventing delusions in walking the inner prayerful life? The Moldavian monk suggested that the devil uses despair as a weapon against us when we pray in our dark nights, much as he would use pride against us when we think we are doing well. The monk quoted Saint Nikitas Stithatos that even if one falls into deep hell, one must never despair, but turn to God and God will restore our strength to carry on, out of hell.

The professor then wondered if a solitary life has any use to the community at all. This is a frequent question we are asked by non-Orthodox (and non-Roman Catholic) faithful. The hermit gave some insights. He said that a hermit does not lead an idle and meaningless life, since he is actually more active than one who is deep in the world. How so? The solitary has to function above his rational self, and has to keep vigil over his being the whole time, observing, logging, analyzing, and praying, all the time. This mental and spiritual activity is much more difficult, especially to maintain on an unceasing manner, than one who is deep in the world, doing many chores. To coin a secular paradigm, a hermit uses many CPU cycles (the central processing unit that is the "heart" of our modern computers) in any one second, than many of us do.

The solitary also shares his insights and findings with us in the world, either by writing (if he observes strict silence), or by occasional conversation. This builds and nurtures us who are in the world, spiritually. And if the solitary leads an exemplary and illuminating life, such a person also serves to inspire the rest of us to lead a faithful life towards God. This is akin to being a lamp to our darkened lives, certainly an important proposition especially in today's clouded and darkened world.

The pilgrim added that even our Lord Jesus Christ stopped teaching or healing others sometimes, and walked away to pray in solitude (St Matthew 14:23, St Luke 6:12).

"Silent solitude is the mother of prayer. It returns one from the imprisonment of sin and allows a subtle growth in virtue, and a slow and steady climb to heaven" - Saint John Climacus (of the Ladder).

Are we spending a "we" time with God daily (Proverbs 8:34, St Luke 9:23)? Or even on a breath-by-breath basis? Every breath we take, in between chores and tasks that demand much of us, do we spend time with God, in inner solitude and silence in the world?

Let us pray, and spend time with God:

> *"Lord Jesus Christ, Son of God,*
> *have mercy on me, a sinner".*

Praying for the needs of others

*Rather than pray just for our own needs,
let us always remember out of faith and
love for God, to remember and pray for
the needs of others.*

Dear beloved,

The professor asked what was the purpose of petitions to God, if God already knew all things, before, during, and after, and His Divine Will being sovereign. Therefore, the professor believed that praying for one another is nothing more than a courtesy out of faith.

The Moldavian monk told the professor, that even if rationally it made sense, perhaps it would be better to use an illustration between two students. One student is lazy and underperforms in all his assignments and examinations. But if a brilliant and hardworking student were to study with the underperforming student, both will benefit from each other. The underperforming student will gain diligence by the influence of the brilliant and hardworking student. And in turn, the brilliant student will learn the virtues of patience and love, and to help the other student become better in his studies.

Therefore, the monk believed that humans are relational creatures, and are best in a community. Therefore, a group of people can nurture and help each other spiritually (Proverbs 17:17). Likewise, prayers to petition God for the needs of others are the same idea, intended for all of us to be purified and to draw closer to God. God certainly does not benefit from our prayers in any way. He acts on our prayers seemingly, when our own limited perspectives make us believe God "reacts" to our needs as we pray. Rather, God's Divine Will has been ahead of us all along.

Praying for the needs of others is Biblical. Our Lord Jesus Christ prayed for His people when He told Apostle Saint Peter that He had prayed for them so that their faith would not fail (St Luke 22:32). And when Saint Peter was thrown into prison, the Body of Christ, the Church, prayed for him. We are also told to confess our sins to one another, and to pray for one another, that we may be healed (St James 5:16, Hebrews 13:18). We are never to neglect the needs of others, out of arrogance like the Pharisees, but to be Christ, washing the feet of His apostles (St Matthew

12:10-12).

We are but sinners, all of us, whether we are deep in the world, deep in piles of gold and silver, deep in the hilltop monasteries, or deep seated in an ecclesial throne (St Luke 6:42, Romans 14:10). Therefore, we as brothers and sisters of one another, are told to strengthen each other, out of faith for our Lord and God, and love for Him and each other, to pray for one another, and to extend our hands in help when we can.

The professor asked, how then can one pray for the needs of others?

The monk added that all prayers, whether confessional and personal in nature towards God, or as a form of intercession for the needs of others, need to be rooted in a real relationship with God, and to the effect of:

"Merciful God, let Your will be done, after Your desire that all of Your children be saved by your Word. Have mercy on Your servant (name), in the name of Jesus Christ our Lord, Amen."

The pilgrim, his spiritual father, the professor, the monk, and the hermit, parted company after a prayer together.

And in conclusion, let us remember that Christ came with a simple reason - Love. We are told to follow His ways, in just one word - Love. When we pursue God with every prayer, let us remember not asking for spiritual gifts, wealth, achievements, but just that God's mercy be on us all (1 Corinthians 13:1-13). Perhaps the representative saint to teach us about a sacrificial love was our beloved Most Holy Theotokos. She loved God with all her heart, without doubt, and she loved others.

Let us pray for all of us, sinners, who are mercifully rested in the grace of our Lord:

> *"Lord Jesus Christ, Son of God,*
> *have mercy on us, sinners".*

PS - This concludes our brief reflection on "The Pilgrim continues his way". We will explore the teachings of Saint Seraphim of Sarov next.

St Seraphim of Sarov's story

Saint Seraphim of Sarov, through the mercy of God, showed humility, deep faith, inner life, wonderworking, and a compassion for all.

Dear beloved,

Saint Seraphim of Sarov was born in Kursk, Russia, in 1759. When he was 10 years old, he fell terribly ill and through the miracle of the Kursk Icon of our beloved Theotokos, he was healed. He spent much of his youth praying, reading Holy Scriptures, attending the Divine Liturgy with faith, and humbly learned from the priests. At 19 years old, he left home and joined the monastery at Sarov, went through a long trial of discipline and testing, was tonsured at 27 years old, ordained a priest at 34 years old, and stayed until his repose in 1833.

In 1804, he was brutally attacked till near death by robbers. His physical ordeal was soothed by the appearance of our beloved Theotokos and the apostles Saint Peter and Saint John to him. He recovered somewhat, but had to rely on a walking stick for the rest of his life with a bent spine (quite a few icons depict the saint this way). Saint Seraphim was deeply pious and once, he knelt on a rock for 1,000 days, praying the Jesus Prayer (St Luke 18:13). The demons relentlessly attacked the saint when he prayed, but could not disturb the saint.

In the last few years of his life, thousands of people came to his cell to learn the inner life of prayer. The saint was a wonderworker, with the Holy Theotokos appearing to him many times, and the saint eventually reposed kneeling in front of an icon of the Theotokos (another commonly shown icon).

Saint Seraphim was attributed to a volume known as "The Little Philokalia", which we will try to extract a little of his sayings here.

The legacy of Saint Seraphim to us in the world was that we must find and rest in the holy mystery of Jesus Christ our Lord. He asked us to revisit the teachings of the early Christians, and to labor through our faith with courage, and relying on God's grace and mercy, to ascend the Ladder.

1. Nature of God? - How do we recognize God? How do we recognize the devil? According to the

saint, there is NO evil where God is. Everything from God must be peaceful, healthy, and invariably leads us to recognizing our sins in humility. To the saint, God is warm, like a fire in the winter. Conversely, only the devil is cold, like the freezing and lifeless winter.

2. How should we love God? - The saint taught us that a person, who has journeyed towards God with a pristine love for Him, will behave as if his own life did not exist, and that he has detached from all his attachments and passions. Such a person would recognize death as a part of life, but would take care of his immortal soul and dedicate his soul to God (St Matthew 16:26).

3. How should we love others? - The saint taught us, that we should be warm and affectionate to others (St Luke 10:27), without any anger or harmful action, for harmful actions and words would weigh down our hearts like lead or rocks. When people are sad or depressed, the saint told us to encourage and cheer them with kind words. When people sin, rather than judge them, we are to cover him, as Saint Isaac the Syrian said, "Stretch out your vestment over the sinner and cover him". The saint taught, that loving others as ourselves show that we love God

truly (St Matthew 10:37).

Let us pray for all of us for the salvation of our Lord:

> *"Lord Jesus Christ, Son of God,*
> *have mercy on us, sinners".*

Mercy & Forgiveness in every step

*Do we smile with tears of joy inside when
we help others? Do we see others as saints,
rather than beasts and demons?*

Dear beloved,

There was once a woman, who lived a good
life. One day, while going to attend the Divine
Liturgy at Church, she was knocked down by a
horse carriage. She managed to get up on her feet,
but her knees were grazed with open wounds. She
went back home, and instead of dressing her
wounds, she aggravated them every day. Over
time, the wounds remained sore, and one day, she
lost her mind. She would then sit by the roadside
every day, cried and wailed uncontrollably
pointing to her open wounds. People on the way
to Church, would see her. Some would take pity
on her and give her a few coins. Others would
ignore her and walked on.

A few years later, an old monk from a remote
monastery passed by; saw the woman, who was
aged by her own doing. The monk saw her
wounds, and said, "matushka, these wounds are

very old, and are merely surface wounds. If you only allow the wounds to heal, you would not have to suffer at your own hands. Yes, the skin would heal and look less perfect than if you were not wounded, but as with life, we learn from our challenges, stand up from our falls, and keep our sight on Christ, and thank God for all His mercies upon us."

A year later, villagers who passed by that road, no longer saw the woman. Apparently, she stopped aggravating her old wounds, allowed them to heal, and started to pray and thank God once again. One might find her at the Divine Liturgy at Church, or tending to her small flower garden in her cottage.

Saint Seraphim of Sarov, despite his suffering and the wretched spine caused by a severe beating by robbers, was a cheerful and humble saint. He would greet all those who came to him for spiritual direction, with much joy. He reminded us, that life is a journey you have to walk anyway. You can choose to be deluded and depressed, or you can choose courageous steps forward, with a meek smile on your face, and a reverent and cheerful heart, knowing that God is with you.

"Cheerfulness is not a sin. It drives away weariness, for from weariness there is sometimes dejection, and there is nothing worse than that" - Saint Seraphim of Sarov.

4. Mercy to the weak - Saint Seraphim was a courageous elder who took on his shoulders to become a starets to the community. He stepped out of his cell to welcome all those who were depressed and dejected by society, lending his warm heart and wise counsel, so that all those depressed who came to him, came to see the light of Christ through the saint's actions and words. To the saint, we in the pastoral labors, are not called to be judges, executioners or ritualists, but most importantly, to fulfill the law of God, that we must be merciful to others as our Father in Heaven is merciful (St Matthew 9:13, St Luke 6:36). When we show mercy to others, we must remember to do it not out of pride, but out of love for God and His creation, who are all one with us.

"If you give anything to him who asks, may the joy of your face precede your alms, and comfort his sorrow with kind words" - Saint Isaac the Syrian.

5. Non-Judgment and Forgiveness - The saint

called us, to show mercy out of love for all through faith in God. At the same time, he reminded us that we should never judge another, even if we see their trespasses against the laws of God. Let us remember the Gospel reminding us to mind the giant log of sin in our own head before we venture to criticize or judge another's pin-sized sin (St Matthew 7:1-5, Romans 14:4).

Christ told us to love our enemies, and never harbor anger or hatred. It is difficult for many of us who are deep in the world. We may face a boss we don't agree with. We may face competitive colleagues who may want our jobs and displace us. We may face neighbors who may not be the best of terms with. We may even have relatives who we hardly meet due to some historical reasons. All these emotional burdens mount up, and through time, become engrained as anger, and eventually, hatred. Sometimes, if we reflect on those ill feelings against others, we may not even remember why we felt that way to begin with.

Yet Christ told us, not to hate our enemies, but love them and do good deeds for them (St Matthew 5:44). What Christ was essentially saying to us, was that we have to transfigure our ill feelings towards others, and transform our own hearts to start with. Imagine a person as an enemy, and it will be impossible to love a person. But if you understand that every single person is a loved creation of God, crafted lovingly by His Holy hands, and that everything in life has a Divine reason beyond our mortal understanding, and that everyone fulfills a Divine purpose of God, then it is more difficult to even see a person as an enemy. If enemies don't really exist, but merely circumstances, wouldn't it be so much easier to love another?

Saint Seraphim of Sarov advised that the reason we do not love others, is because we don't even take time to learn about ourselves. He said that if we are busy learning about our own shortcomings, we wouldn't even have time to notice the shortcomings of others. He said by judging ourselves, we would stop judging others. He told us, to judge deeds, but not the doer. His most direct and powerful advice was that we should deem ourselves the WORST sinners of all. The good saint also said that the door of penitence is always open. We have seen this on the Crucifixion of Christ and the two thieves. The thief who asked Christ to remember him when

Christ ascended, and Christ immediately said, "In truth I tell you, today you will be with me in paradise" (St Luke 23:43).

Therefore, salvation is not culminated at the Mystery of baptism and chrismation, but is a lifelong struggle towards God right to the last breath we take before death. If that is so, let us always be our most honest mirror to our sins, so that we may step ever closer to God, and not stray away because we chose instead to shine our critical light on others.

Let us pray, my beloved:

"Lord Jesus Christ, Son of God,
have mercy on me, a sinner."

Power of a penitent & humble heart

Holy Scripture gave us the roadmap to God, and specifically, calling us to always have a penitent and humble heart, that prays and calls to God in all things.

Dear beloved,

There were two families living next to each other. Both families had one boy each. The boys were of the same age, five. The Ivanovs were pious and strict, and their boy Pavel was obedient, pious, and eager to learn. Conversely, the Popovs, though pious and hardworking had no time for their boy, Yakov. Being left to his own devices, Yakov was unruly and disinterested.

Pavel's parents were hard at work, but spent time with their son to educate the boy to be prayerful, to be respectful of all elders, to acquire an appetite for reading and writing, and to be conscientious. Pavel did not simply listen when his parents were around, but his heart was one of surrendering his own will to that of his parents, because he trusted in the best judgment and wisdom of his parents.

Conversely, Yakov's parents had no time with him, and he hated reading or writing, and was often rude to his own parents and relatives, and even scolded or beaten elders without his parents bothering to intervene. Yakov did not listen to anyone, and his will overrode his parents', who were powerless to do much with him.

Twenty years later, Pavel graduated from a top university as an engineer, and was employed in an international corporation, and was soon to marry a lady who was pious and hardworking. Pavel remained obedient to the wishes of his parents, and more importantly, he always kept his faith and complete trust in God.

However, Yakov was not having a good time. He dropped out of school against the wishes of his parents. When he was fourteen, he joined a gang and caused much heartache to his parents. He was caught by the police trying to rob an establishment, and spent his youth in prison. When he was released, he could not find a job and stayed with his parents. But yet he did not learn his lesson, and his parents aged terribly trying to give in to his needs. Eventually, his father died from a stroke and his mother soon after.

6. True Repentance - Saint Seraphim of Sarov instructed us to have a humble and penitent heart always (Psalm 51:19). When a heart is full of humility and repentance, it is not just a constant whipping of oneself over sins and sinking into deep depression, but a surrendering of one's will to God completely. The devil is adept at twisting our emotions and passions, and depression is one of the tools of his trickery. But when we surrender our entire will to God as a prostration of our submission out of love, God takes the burden of inner hell from us. It does require us to, out of true humility, bare our raw inner hell to God, and say meekly to Him, "Lord, I bare my true sins, a burden of hell too painful for me to carry. Please take this from me." God, in His unmistakable infinite mercy, takes our burdens and sins away because we allow His will be done.

God's love is a constant bright sun, that gives us warmth when we release our wills and burdens to Him out of love, and in turn, His light of love permeates throughout our bodies and spirits, and we find incredible comfort and peace. Conversely, if we stubbornly choose to fortify our own wills and sins and stand defiantly against Him, then His infinite love will seem to burn through our bodies and spirits as if we are in hell. His love and grace is the same, it is merely us who need to make an active step towards Him to experience His love as He intends it to be.

7. All in good time - God is infinite, and not bound by time and space (Romans 8:18). Conversely, due to our limited spatial perception and lifespan, our perception of time and space are very myopic. All too often, we are obsessed by our own passions, that we become blind to His everyday mercy in subtle and not so subtle forms. We keep wondering why our passions and desires are not fulfilled, even as we "pray" frequently. However, it is not God's plan to satiate our every desire, but rather, He will fulfill a greater Divine plan to draw us closer to Him in salvation and eternal life. Therefore, what we want (as a function of lust) is totally opposite to what God want for us (as a function of love and salvation).

Saint Seraphim also advised us, to take all insults, humiliation or injustice in silence, and only confess our pains to God (St Luke 6:30). This is not easy, and for many of us, almost impossible to swallow. Christ, the Perfecter of our faith in God, did not lead us on an easy and wide path. He told us certainly, that the path to God is a narrow and difficult one. After all, if one can fight tooth and nail over mere gold and silver, what would one expect of the priceless gifts of salvation and eternal life? Therefore, when Christ asked us to love God and others, the premise is love. If you can love someone truly, you would never see insults or shame, but counsel and wisdom.

"Humble yourself and you will see the glory of God within yourself" - Saint Isaac the Syrian.

8. Keeping our hearts safe - The Book of Proverbs gave us lots of wisdom to daily life, including that of keeping our hearts safe from the assaults of the evil one (Proverbs 4:23). Although we sometimes hear of suppressing our evil and unclean thoughts as they surface. However, our strength is feeble, and our wills weak, so let us remember our greatest defense against such thoughts - surrendering ourselves to God's will, through the prayer of the heart.

As we pray unceasingly unto Him, layers and layers of grime and dirt fall away, revealing more and more of Him within us. "Blessed are the pure in heart, for they shall see God" (St Matthew 5:8).

The evil one will gnaw at us at all times, in many guises. He can come as tempters in physical form, or he can tempt us from within. The more we safeguard our hearts in a pristine prayer and nothing else, the less he can assault us with his tricks. In a still lake frozen in permanent prayer, there is nothing the evil one can do. But if our hearts are tumultuous in evil thoughts and sins like a raging sea, there is much he can tempt, much he can steal, and much he can destroy.

Let us pray, beloved, out of a pure heart, wishing nothing except the rest from God,

*"Lord Jesus Christ, Son of God,
have mercy on me, a sinner".*

Heart of a pilgrim in action

A pilgrim need not be in the desert, but deep in the world, leading a seeking, prayerful, and humble life.

Dear beloved,

Let me tell you a story of Abba Achilles, a Desert Father.

Three old men came to Abba Achilles and asked a favor from the holy father.

The first old man asked, "Father, please make a fishing net for me." Abba Achilles replied, "No, I will not make you one."

The second old man asked, "Father, please make a fishing net for me out of charity, so that we may have a souvenir of you of the monastery." Abba Achilles replied, "No, I do not have time."

The third old man, with a bad reputation, asked, "Father, please make me a fishing net so that I have something from your hands." Abba Achilles replied, "For you, I will make one."

The other two old men were perturbed and

asked privately, why the Abba would make a fishing net for the old man with the bad reputation, but not the two of them.

Abba Achilles replied, "I did not make a fishing net for each of you, because you would believe I have no time. But if I did not make a fishing net for him, he would have thought that I am aware of his sins and thus denied him the request. That would have broken down our relationship. Now, I have cheered his soul and he would not be filled with grief."

Therefore, we in the pastoral labors have to understand that as spiritual elders, much as Abba Achilles and Saint Seraphim of Sarov demonstrated, that love much always go before our steps, and that we must keep vigil of our actions so that those who seek our counsel, can be filled with joy for the Lord, and not feel rejected. We were called as humble servants of the Lord, not masters.

9. Movements of the heart - Saint Seraphim taught us, that the differentiator between the signs of God, and the signs of the evil one, is what we experience from the signs. When we accept anything from God, we can only experience joy in

our hearts. But when we accept things from the devil, no matter how sugarcoated it was presented to us, the fruits are always bitter, and will torment us. The spiritual fruits of a heart truly resting in the Lord feels love, joy, peace, long suffering, gentleness, goodness, faith, meekness, and temperance (Galatians 5:22-23).

Be not deceived by the signs and fruits of the evil one, for he stalks us, assaults us relentlessly especially if we are seeking God (Psalm 9:29). He would even present himself as an angel of light. That is why, we are told be keep vigil, and discern all thoughts and feelings within us, release our burdens unto God, and pray with a penitent and humble heart.

Saint Seraphim described the difference between a pure heart, and an impure heart. The pure heart has transfigured the passions so that the evil one can only touch indirectly or externally. However, the impure heart is filled with unclean passions, and the evil one can twist and distort the impure heart internally and strip the person of any attempt of reaching God. This is why the discernment and transfiguration of passions is so important, and that only with repentant and humble heart of tears can we ask

God to take away our passions and fill us with a joyful resting in Him.

10. An active contemplative - Saint Seraphim taught that since a person has two parts, a soul, and a body, so the spiritual pilgrimage must be a synergy of two things - physical activities (active), and spiritual activities (contemplative).

An active life that draws us closer to God refer to fasting, abstinence, prayer, attending the Divine Liturgy, good deeds, etc, which are meant as a spiritual discipline that would lead us to Him (St Matthew 7:14).

A contemplative life that draws us closer to God are the inner life, the prayerful life "in the closet", that requires us to discern, examine, reflect, and pray unceasingly.

Saint Seraphim taught that the active life must precede the contemplative life. We must not short-circuit our spiritual path or progression by jumping into the contemplative life without first walking diligently and humbly, the active life. This is because the active life helps us to transfigure our passions, and slowly and steadily lead us to a cleaner contemplative path (St Matthew 5:8).

"Only those who are perfect by their experience can without danger proceed to contemplation" - Saint Gregory of Nazianzus, father among the saints.

We are advised by the Holy Fathers to seek out a good spiritual director who will guide us along both the active and contemplative lives. If we cannot find one, do not despair, but pray with tears to God to guide us through the Holy Scriptures (St John 5:39).

Let us pray, beloved, for the strength and mercy of God, when we struggle to transfigure our passions towards Him,

> *"Lord Jesus Christ, Son of God,*
> *have mercy on me, a sinner."*

The Little Rule of St Seraphim

*This daily prayer rule is attributed to
Saint Pachomius of Egypt, said to be given
to him by an angel of the Lord. Saint
Seraphim of Sarov often taught this to
many of his spiritual children.*

In the name of Father, Son [+], and Holy Spirit, Amen.

Glory to Thee, O God, glory to Thee.

Heavenly King, Comforter, Spirit of Truth, Who art everywhere present and fillest all things, Treasury of good gifts, and Giver of life, come and abide in us, and cleanse us of all impurity, and save our souls, O Good One.

Holy God, Holy Mighty [+], Holy Immortal, have mercy on us. (3 times)

Glory to Father, Son [+], and Holy Spirit, now and ever, and unto ages of ages. Amen.

Most Holy Trinity, have mercy on us. Lord, cleanse our sins. Master, pardon our iniquities. Holy One, visit and heal our infirmities for Thy name's sake.

Lord, have mercy. (3 times)

Glory to Father, Son [+], and Holy Spirit, now and ever, and unto ages of ages. Amen.

Our Father, Who art in the heavens, hallowed be Thy name. Thy kingdom come, Thy will be done, on earth as it is in heaven. Give us this day our daily bread, and forgive our debts, as we forgive our debtors. And lead us not into temptation, but deliver us from the evil-one.

Through the prayers of our holy Fathers, Lord Jesus Christ our God, have mercy on us. Amen.

Lord, have mercy. (12 times)

Glory to Father, Son [+], and Holy Spirit, now and ever, and unto ages of ages. Amen.

O come, let us worship God our King. O come, let us worship and fall down before Christ, our King and God. O come, let us worship and fall down before Christ Himself, our King and God.

Psalm 50

Have mercy on me, O God, according to Thy great mercy; and according to the multitude of Thy compassions blot out my transgression. Wash me thoroughly from mine iniquity, and cleanse me from my sin. For I know mine iniquity, and my sin is ever before me. Against Thee only have I sinned and done this evil before Thee, that Thou mightest be justified in Thy words, and prevail when Thou art judged. For behold, I was conceived in iniquities, and in sins did my mother bear me. For behold, Thou hast loved truth; the hidden and secret things of Thy wisdom hast Thou made manifest unto me. Thou shalt sprinkle me with hyssop, and I shall be made clean; Thou shalt wash me, and I shall be made whiter than snow. Thou shalt make me to hear joy and gladness; the bones that be humbled, they shall rejoice. Turn Thy face away from my sins, and blot out all mine iniquities. Create in me a clean heart, O God, and renew a right spirit within me. Cast me not away from Thy presence, and take not Thy Holy Spirit from me. Restore unto me the joy of Thy salvation, and with Thy governing Spirit establish me. I shall teach transgressors Thy ways, and the ungodly shall turn back unto Thee. Deliver me from blood-guiltiness, O God, Thou God of my salvation; my tongue shall rejoice in Thy righteousness. O Lord, Thou shalt open my lips, and my mouth shall declare Thy praise. For if Thou hadst desired sacrifice, I had given it; with whole-burnt offerings Thou shalt not be pleased. A sacrifice unto God is a broken spirit; a heart that is broken and humbled God will not despise. Do good, O Lord, in Thy good pleasure unto Zion, and let the walls of Jerusalem be built. Then shalt Thou be pleased with a sacrifice of righteousness, with oblation and whole-burnt offerings. Then shall they offer bullocks upon Thine altar.

The Creed

I believe in one God, the Father Almighty, Maker of heaven and earth and of all things visible and invisible. And in one Lord Jesus Christ, the Son of God, the Only-begotten, begotten of the Father before all ages; Light of Light, true God of true God; begotten, not made; of one essence with the Father, by Whom all things were made; Who for us men and for our salvation came down from the heavens, and was incarnate of the Holy Spirit and the Virgin Mary, and became man; And was crucified for us under Pontius Pilate, and suffered and was buried; And arose again on the third day according to the Scriptures; And ascended into the heavens, and sits at the right hand of the Father; And shall come again, with glory, to judge both the living and the dead; Whose kingdom shall have no end.

And in the Holy Spirit, the Lord, the Giver of life; Who proceeds from the Father; Who with the Father and the Son together is worshipped and glorified; Who spake by the prophets. In One, Holy, Catholic, and Apostolic Church. I confess one baptism for the remission of sins. I look for the resurrection of the dead, And the life of the age to come. Amen.

Jesus Prayer

Lord Jesus Christ, Son of God, have mercy on me, a sinner. (100 times)

Thanksgiving

It is truly meet to call thee blest, the Theotokos, ever blessed and most pure, and the Mother of our God. More honorable than the Cherubim, and more glorious than the Seraphim, without corruption thou gavest birth to God the Word: True Theotokos, we magnify thee. O virgin Theotokos, rejoice; O Mary full of grace, the Lord is with thee. Blessed art thou among women, and blessed is the fruit of thy womb, for thou hast borne the Savior of our souls, Jesus Christ our Lord. Amen. (3 times)

Glory to Father, Son [+], and Holy Spirit, now

and ever, and unto ages of ages. Amen.

Lord, have mercy. (3 times)

O Lord, Bless. O Lord Jesus Christ, Son of God, through the prayers of Thy most pure Mother, of our holy and God-bearing fathers, and all the saints, have mercy on us and save us, for Thou art good and the Lover of mankind. Amen.

The Didache

The Didache, or the "Teaching of the 12 Apostles to the Gentiles", is an ancient document, considered by many, to be a summary of the New Testament. The document has 16 short chapters, separated into 4 parts.

1. Way of Life and the Way of Death (ch 1-6);

2. Baptism, Fasting, and Communion (ch 7-10);

3. Ministry and Traveling Prophets (ch 11-15);

4. Brief Apocalypse (ch 16).

Didache Part 1: Way of Life & Death

1:1 There are two paths that differ greatly, one of life and one of death.

1:2 The path of life is this. First, love God who made you, love others as yourself, and never do things to others that you would not want others to do to you.

1:3 And the doctrine of these maxims is as follows. Bless them that curse you, and pray for your enemies. Fast on behalf of those that persecute you; for what thanks is there if you love them that love you? Do not even the Gentiles do the same? But love them that hate you, and you will not have an enemy.

1:4 Abstain from fleshly and worldly lusts. If anyone give you a blow on your right cheek, turn unto him the other also, and you shall be perfect; if anyone compel you to go a mile, go with him two miles; if a man takes away your cloak, give him your coat also; if a man takes from you what is yours, ask not for it again, for neither are you able to do so.

1:5 Give to everyone that asks of you, and ask

not again; for the Father wishes that from His own gifts there should be given to all. Blessed is he who gives according to the commandment, for he is free from guilt; but woe unto him that receives. For if a man receives being in need, he shall be free from guilt; but he who receives when not in need, shall pay a penalty as to why he received and for what purpose; and when he is in tribulation he shall be examined concerning the things that he has done, and shall not depart thence until he has paid the last coin.

1:6 For of a truth it has been said on these matters, let your almsgiving abide in your hands until you know to whom you have given.

2 of 16

2:1 But the second commandment of the teaching is this.

2:2 Do not kill; do not commit adultery; do not corrupt the youth; do not commit fornication; do not steal; do not use soothsaying; do not practice sorcery; do not kill a child by abortion or when born; do not covet things of other people.

2:3 Do not commit perjury; do not bear false

witness; do not speak evil; do not bear malice.

2:4 Do not be double-minded (unstable) or double-tongued, for to be such is the snare of death.

2:5 Your speech shall not be false or empty, but concerned with action.

2:6 Do not be covetous, or greedy, or hypocritical, or malicious, or proud; do not plot against others;

2:7 Do not hate anyone; but some you may prove to be wrong, some others you shall pray for, and some you shall love beyond your own soul.

3 of 16

3:1 My beloved, fly from everything that is evil or even any semblance of evil.

3:2 Do not be angry, for anger leads to slaughter; be not jealous, or contentious, or quarrelsome, for from all these things slaughter ensues.

3:3 Do not be lustful, for lust leads to fornication; be not a filthy talker; do not lift up your eyes, for from all these things lead to adultery.

3:4 Do not observe omens, since it leads to idolatry; nor a user of spells, nor an astrologer, nor a traveling purifier, nor wish to see these things, for from all these things lead to idolatry.

3:5 Do not lie, for lying leads to theft; be not covetous or conceited, for from all these things lead to theft.

3:6 Do not gossip, since it leads to blasphemy; be not self-willed or evil-minded, for from all these things lead to blasphemy.

3:7 But my beloved, be meek, for the meek shall inherit the earth.

3:8 Be longsuffering, compassionate, harmless, peaceable, good, and fearing always the Word of God that you have heard.

3:9 Do not exalt yourself or embolden your soul. You soul shall not be joined with the arrogant ones, but you shall walk with the just and humble.

3:10 Accept all things that happen to you as good, since without God nothing happens.

4:1 My beloved, remember both night and day anyone who speaks to you the Word of God; honor such a person as you would the Lord, for where the teaching of the Lord is given, there is the Lord.

4:2 Seek out day by day the wisdom of the saints that you may rest in their words.

4:3 Do not desire schism, but set at peace people who contend; judge righteously; do not accept the person of anyone to convict a person of transgression.

4:4 Do not doubt whether a thing shall be or not.

4:5 Do not be one who is so ready to receive, but so reluctant to give.

4:6 If you can, give by means of you hands as a redemption for your sins.

4:7 Do not doubt or gossip about others when giving; for you know the Lord is the fair recompenser of the reward.

4:8 Do not turn away from those who are in need, but share with your brother in all things, and do not say that things are your own; for if you are partners in what is immortal, how much more in what is mortal?

4:9 Put your heart into teaching your sons and daughters, so they will learn the fear of God.

4:10 Do not command with bitterness those who labor for you, who hope in the same God as you, lest they fear not in consequence God who is over both; for Christ came and called us to respect all whom the Holy Spirit has prepared.

4:11 And for those who labor for their superiors, submit yourselves to your superiors with reverence and fear, seeing them as an image of God.

4:12 Hate all hypocrisy and everything that is not pleasing to God.

4:13 Do not abandon the commandments of the Lord, but guard His Truth that you have received, neither adding nor subtracting therefrom.

4:14 Confess thy transgressions in the Church, and do not come to prayer with an evil conscience. This is the path of life.

5:1 But the path of death is this. First of all, it is evil, and full of cursing; there are murders, adulteries, lusts, fornication, thefts, idolatries, soothsaying, sorceries, robberies, false witnessing, hypocrisies, double-mindedness, craft, pride, malice, self-will, covetousness, filthy talking, jealousy, audacity, pride, and arrogance.

5:2 There are people who persecute the good - lovers of a lie, not knowing the reward of righteousness, not cleaving to the good nor to righteous judgment, watching not for the good but for the evil, from whom meekness and patience are absent, loving things that are vain, hungry after rewards, having no compassion for the needy, nor laboring for those in trouble, not knowing God who made them, murderers of children, corrupters of the image of God, who turn away from those in need, who oppress those in trouble, unjust judges of the poor, erring in all things. From all these, my beloved, may you be delivered.

6:1 Keep vigilant so that no one will make you err from this path of doctrine, since one who does so is tearing you apart from God.

6:2 If you can bear the whole yoke of the Lord, you will be perfect; but if you are not able, do what you are able.

6:3 But concerning meat, bear that which you are able to do. But be aware of food sacrificed to idols, for it is the worship of the infernal deities.

Didache Part 2: Baptism Fasting & Communion

7:1 Baptize people in this manner. Having first recited all the precepts, baptize in the name of the Father, and of the Son, and of the Holy Spirit, in running water.

7:2 If you do not have running water, baptize in some other water. If you do not have cold water, you can use warm water.

7:3 If you do not have all these, pour water three times on the head, in the name of the Father, and of the Son, and of the Holy Spirit.

7:4 Before the baptism, let him who baptizes and him who is to be baptized fast previously, and any others who are able. Command him who is to be baptized to fast one or two days before.

8:1 Do not fast like the hypocrites, for they fast on the second and fifth days of the week, but you shall fast on the fourth and sixth days instead.

8:2 Do not pray as the hypocrites, but pray as the Lord has commanded in His Gospel: "Our Father, Who art in the heavens, hallowed be Thy name. Thy kingdom come, Thy will be done, on earth as it is in heaven. Give us this day our daily bread, and forgive our debts, as we forgive our debtors. And lead us not into temptation, but deliver us from the evil-one: for Thine is the power, and the glory, for ever."

8:3 Pray this way three times a day.

9 of 16

9:1 Give thanks in the Eucharist in this fashion.

9:2 First, concerning the cup. We thank Thee, our Father, for the holy vine, David Thy Son, which Thou have made known to us through Jesus Christ Thy Son; to Thee be the glory forever.

9:3 And concerning the broken bread. We thank Thee, our Father, for the life and knowledge that Thou have made known to us through Jesus Christ Thy Son; to Thee be the glory forever.

9:4 As this broken bread was once scattered on the mountains, and after it had been brought together became one, so may Thy Church be gathered together from the ends of the earth unto Thy kingdom; for Thine is the glory, and the power, through Jesus Christ, forever.

9:5 And let none eat or drink of your Eucharist but such as have been baptized into the name of the Lord, for of a truth the Lord has said concerning this, give not that which is holy to the dogs.

10 of 16

10:1 After it has been completed, pray this way.

10:2 We thank Thee, Holy Father, for Thy Holy Name, which Thou hast caused to dwell in our hearts, and for the knowledge and faith and immortality that Thou hast made known unto us through Jesus Christ Thy Son; to Thee be the glory forever.

10:3 Almighty Master, Who didst create all things for the sake of Thy Name, and hast given both meat and drink, for men to enjoy, that we might give thanks unto Thee, but to us Thou hast given spiritual meat and drink, and life everlasting, through Thy Son.

10:4 Above all, we thank Thee that Thou art able to save; to Thee be the glory forever.

10:5 Remember, Lord, Thy Church, to redeem it from every evil, and to perfect it in Thy love, and gather it together from the four winds, even that which has been sanctified for Thy kingdom which Thou hast prepared for it; for Thine is the kingdom and the glory forever.

10:6 Let grace come, and let this world pass away. Hosanna to the Son of David. If anyone is holy let him come to the Eucharist; if anyone is not, let him repent. Maranatha. Amen.

10:7 Let the prophets give thanks, so far as they are willing to do so.

11:1 Receive whoever shall come and teach you all these things we have said before (in earlier chapters).

11:2 Reject a teacher who subverts and teaches you a conflicting doctrine. Receive a teacher as the Lord Himself, if he comes to add to your righteousness, and the knowledge of the Lord.

11:3 But concerning the apostles and prophets, do all things according to the doctrine of the Gospel.

11:4 Let every apostle who come to you be received as the Lord.

11:5 Such an apostle will remain one day, and if it be necessary, a second day; but if he remains three days, he is a false prophet.

11:6 And let the apostle when departing take nothing but bread until he arrives at his resting place; but if he asks for money, he is a false prophet.

11:7 Do not tempt or dispute with any prophet who speaks in the Holy Spirit; for every sin shall be forgiven, but this sin shall not be forgiven.

11:8 But not everyone who speaks in the spirit is a prophet, but he is so who has the disposition of the Lord; by their dispositions they therefore shall be known, the false prophet and the prophet.

11:9 And every prophet who orders in the Holy Spirit that a table shall be laid, shall not eat of it himself. But if he do otherwise, he is a false prophet.

11:10 Every prophet who teaches the Truth, but does not do what he preaches, is a false prophet.

11:11 Every prophet who is approved and true, and ministering in the visible mystery of the Church, but who teaches not others to do the things that he does himself, shall not be judged by you, for with God lies his judgment, for in this manner also did the ancient prophets.

11:12 But whoever shall say in the spirit, give me money, or things of that kind, listen not to him; but if he tell you concerning others that are in need that you should give unto them, let no one judge him.

12:1 Let everyone who comes in the Name of the Lord be received, but afterwards examine him and know his character, for you have knowledge both of good and evil.

12:2 If a traveler comes to you, assist him as much as you are able; but he will not remain with you more than two or three days, unless there be a necessity.

12:3 If a person who is a craftsman wishes to settle with you, let him work, and so eat.

12:4 But if a person who comes to you knows not any craft, provide according to your own discretion, but know that a Christian may not live idle among you.

12:5 But reject those unskilled who are unwilling to work for a fair wage and yet expect you to provide.

13:1 Every true prophet who is willing to dwell among you is worthy of his meat.

13:2 Likewise a true teacher is himself worthy of his meat, even as is a laborer.

13:3 Take the first fruits of every produce of the winepress and threshing-floor, of oxen and sheep, and give it to the prophets, for they are your chief priests.

13:4 But if you do not have a prophet, give it to the poor.

13:5 If you prepare a feast, take and give the first fruits according to the commandment of God.

13:6 In the same manner, when you open a jar of wine or oil, take the first fruits and give it to the prophets.

13:7 Take also the first fruits of money, of clothes, and of every possession, as it shall seem good to you, and give it according to the commandment of God.

14:1 But on the Lord's day, after you have assembled together, confess your sins so that your sacrifice may be pure, break bread and give thanks.

14:2 Let those who have had a quarrel with others be reconciled first, before they attend the assembly, so that your sacrifice may not be polluted.

14:3 For the Lord said, "In every place and time offer unto me a pure sacrifice, for I am a great King, saith the Lord, and my name is wonderful among the Gentiles."

15:1 Elect bishops and deacons worthy of the Lord, men who are meek and not covetous, true and approved, for they perform for you the service of prophets and teachers.

15:2 Do not despise them, for they are those who are honored among you, together with the prophets and teachers.

15:3 Rebuke one another, not in anger but in

peace, as the Gospel commanded you. Let no one speak to anyone who walks disorderly with regards to his neighbor, neither let him be heard by you until he first repents.

15:4 Pray, give alms, and in all your deeds, do as the Gospel of our Lord commanded you.

Didache Part 4: Brief Apocalypse

16:1 Watch concerning your life; let not your lamps be quenched or your loins be loosed, but be ready, for you do not know the hour at which our Lord comes.

16:2 Gather together frequently, seeking what is suitable for your souls; for the whole time of your faith shall profit you not, unless you are found perfect in the last time.

16:3 For in the last days false prophets and seducers shall be multiplied, and the sheep shall be turned into wolves, and love shall be turned into hate.

16:4 And because iniquity is abundant people shall hate and persecute each other, and deliver each other up; and then the Deceiver of the world appear as the Son of God, and shall do signs and wonders, and the earth shall be delivered into his hands; and he shall do unlawful things, such as have never happened since the beginning of the world.

16:5 Then shall the creation of man come to the fiery trial of proof, and many shall be offended and shall perish; but they who remain in their faith shall be saved by the rock of offence itself.

16:6 And then shall appear the signs of the truth; first the sign of the appearance in heaven, then the sign of the sound of the trumpet, and thirdly the resurrection of the dead.

16:7 Not of all, but as it has been said, the Lord shall come and all His saints with Him;

16:8 Then shall the world behold the Lord coming on the clouds of heaven.

{End}

Not copyrighted, Athenaeum of Christian Antiquity. Trans: Charles H Hoole. Ed: Friar Martin Fontenot Gonzalez, St Pachomius Library, 10/1994.
Contemporary Language adapted by: Father Raphael, 12/2010.

More information

Father Raphael (Seamus Phan), is a priest, spiritual director, writer, and software developer. He is a bivocational "tent-making" priest. His interests include pre-Nicene Christianity, early Christian writings (such as the Desert Fathers), liturgies, hesychasm, and philosophies.

If you like to learn more about the writing apostolate of Father Raphael, and his pastoral labors as a spiritual director and priest, please visit:

www.saintflannan.org

www.ingramcontent.com/pod-product-compliance
Lightning Source LLC
LaVergne TN
LVHW051054080426
835508LV00019B/1878